Prayers
for the
Classroom

Philip A. Verhalen
Editor

Foreword by
Archbishop Rembert G. Weakland, O.S.B.

A Liturgical Press Book

THE LITURGICAL PRESS
Collegeville, Minnesota

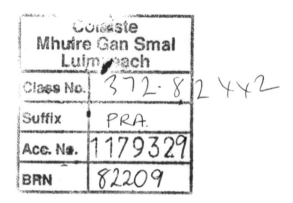
Cover design by Ann Blattner

1   2   3   4   5   6   7   8

Library of Congress Cataloging-in-Publication Data

Prayers for the classroom / Philip A. Verhalen, editor ; foreword by
   Rembert G. Weakland.
      p.   cm.
   Includes bibliographical references and index.
   ISBN 0-8146-2456-1 (alk. paper)
   1. Schools—Prayers. I. Verhalen, Philip A.
BV283.S3P74   1998
264'.13—dc21
                                                      97-27348
                                                        CIP

Dedicated to
the Bellarmine Community
of Tacoma

Contents

Foreword

We are all blessed by the fact that the disciples had the courage to ask Jesus how to pray. We know that praying should be like breathing, just a normal part of our daily lives. Yet, we need help, like those first disciples. Jesus' answer was to give us the Our Father. It remains the model of the perfect prayer. It begins by calling on God as our loving and caring parent. Only then do we talk about our daily needs and gain the courage we must have to face the daily round of ups and downs. We believe that God is with us.

Often, however, when we try to pray, we find ourselves dry and empty. On those occasions we need to fall back on the example that others have given us. We learn from their reliance on God, from their admission of need, from their deep faith and trust that God loves them, is with them and hears them. Every prayer is a variation of the Our Father.

These prayers gathered by Philip A. Verhalen can be of immense help to all. From them we can learn how to pray both with others as well as on our own. So many of the examples are perfect models for us both when we pray together as well as when we pray alone and in the private depths of our inner selves. They are ways in which the whole group can join together, since they go beyond the whims of the personal and include the needs of the whole group. They have about them a sense of the universal. They have been tried and tested.

Even then we should know that being one with Jesus Christ means that we are still one with each other. Thus, they teach us how to pray even when we are by ourselves and feel in deep need. Many of these prayers are also very personal in that they touch our hearts.

My own prayer is that they will be used by many, that they will stimulate the minds and hearts of those who use them to a greater union with God, one that leads to the kind of spontaneous prayer that comes from the depths of the inner-self, and that they will then become like breathing, just a natural part of everyone's existence.

We still ask: "Lord, teach us to pray." The answer is always the same: "Rely on me as a loving parent, ask for what you need. Trust. My love will not diminish."

Archbishop Rembert G. Weakland, O.S.B.

Acknowledgments

The Scripture quotations are from the New Revised Standard Version Bible, Catholic edition, © 1989 by the Division of Christian Education of the National Council of Churches of Christ in the USA. Used by permission. All rights reserved.

Appleton, George. *One Man's Prayers.* London: S.P.C.K. Reprinted in *Oxford Book of Prayers,* No. 460.

Appleton, George, general editor. *The Oxford Book of Prayers.* New York: Oxford University Press, 1985, Nos. 15, 211, 422, 926, 954.

Carden, John (ed.). *Morning, Noon, Night.* London: Church Missionary Society, Partnership House, 1976. Reprinted in *Oxford Book of Prayers,* Nos. 377, 420, 905.

The Collected Poems of G. K. Chesterton. New York: Dodd, Mead and Co., Inc., 1980, pp. 136, 137.

Editors of Conari Press. *Random Acts of Kindness.* Emeryville, Calif.: Conari Press, 1993, pp. 19, 47, 53.

Farjeon, Eleanor, "Morning Has Broken," from *The Children's Bells,* reprinted with permission of David Higham Associates Limited, London.

Foss, Michael, ed., *Poetry of the World Wars.* New York: Peter Bedrick Books, Inc., 1990, p. 114.

Frost, Robert. "The Road Not Taken," *The Poetry of Robert Frost.* New York: Henry Holt and Company, Inc., 1969.

Fulghum, Robert. *All I Really Need to Know I Learned in Kindergarten.* © 1986, 1988 by Robert L. Fulghum. Reprinted with permission of Villard Books, a division of Random House.

de Gasztold, Carmen Bernos. "The Prayer of the Tortoise," from *Prayers from the Ark.* Translated by Rumer Godden. Translation © 1962, Renewed 1990 by Rumer Godden. Original © 1947, © 1955 by Editions du Cloitre. Used by permission of Viking Penguin, a division of Penguin Books, U.S.A., Inc.

Hanh, Thich Nhat. "A Buddhist Litany for Peace" 1976 and "Water Prayer." Reprinted from *Present Moment Wonderful Moment: Mindfulness Verses for Daily Living* 1990, with permission of Paralax Press, Berkeley, California.

Harter, Michael, S.J. (ed.). *Hearts on Fire.* St. Louis: The Institute of Jesuit Sources, 1993, p. 29.

Holland, Margaret. "A Christmas Meditation," reprinted with permission of the author.

Johnson, Thomas H., ed. *Final Harvest: Emily Dickinson's Poems.* Boston: Little, Brown and Co.: 1961, pp. 221, 372.

Lathem, Edward Connery, ed. *The Poetry of Robert Frost.* New York: Holt, Rinehart and Winston, 1969, p. 105.

Link, Mark. *Vision 2000.* Allen, Texas: Tabor Publishers, 1992, pp. 15, 19, 39, 51, 106.

De Mello, Anthony, S.J. *The Song of the Bird.* Gujaret, India: Sahitya Prakash Anand, 1982, pp. 4, 5, 9, 12, 13, 18, 19, 39, 46, 47, 76, 77, 108, 109, 142, 143.

Micklen, Caryl (ed.). *Contemporary Prayers for Public Worship.* London: S.C.M. Press, 1967. Reprinted in *Oxford Book of Prayers,* No. 526.

Roberts, Elizabeth, and Elias Amidon, eds. *Earth Prayers.* San Francisco: Harper Collins Publishers, 1991, pp. 69, 92, 106, 118, 139, 154, 160, 179, 198, 222, 381.

Rossetti, Christina. *Selected Poems,* "My Gift." Reprinted with permission of Carcanet Press Limited, Manchester, England.

Sisson, C.H., ed. *Christina Rossetti: Selected Poems.* Manchester, England: Carcanet Press, Ltd., 1984, pp. 126, 127.

Sister Ruth Prayer. Reprinted with permission of S.L.G. Press, Convent of the Incarnation, Fairacres, Oxford, England. Found in *Oxford Book of Prayers.*

Southern Bushman Prayers. Reprinted with permission of the National Museum and Art Gallery, Botswana. Translated by Black and Lloyd; later transposed into verse by Arthur Markowitz in *The Rebirth of an Ostrich.*

Uhlein, Gabrielle. *Meditations With Hildegard of Bingen.* Santa Fe: Bear and Company, Inc., 1983. Reprinted with permission.

Untermeyer, Louis, ed. *A Treasury of Great Poems.* Vol. II. New York: Simon and Schuster, 1955, pp. 640, 650, 705, 710, 723, 781, 809, 827, 829, 837, 861, 893, 894, 923, 926, 927, 928, 947, 978, 1002, 1003, 1034, 1035, 1049, 1098, 1118, 1146, 1205.

Winter, Miriam Therese. *Woman Word.* New York: Crossroads Publishing Co., 1991, pp. 27, 43, 160.

I want to extend my warmest thanks to my students over the last several years for their honest feedback to the development of this book, and to Judy Iverson and Gary Dillon who diligently put the total work in a practical and readable form. Also, special thanks to Archbishop Rembert Weakland, O.S.B., for his warm welcoming message preparing the reader for the role of this book.

Like so much in life, I am grateful for the solid support of friends in the background, especially: my immediate family, Jim, Flo, Rosie, and Charlie; my in-laws, Jay and Sue, and all the Quinn family; my dear friend John Olivier; Jeanne Dressel, for her personal and candid critique of the content; Rita Kowatts, for her design; Jake Zimmerman; Walt and Margie Babb; Darrell and Lucy Reeck; Peg and Joe Haggerty; Marian Leonard; Lynn Davis; Ray and Marian Malonson; Jim Goodwin, S.J.; Dale Turner; and so many others who provided background awareness of this production, and finally Kathy, my wife, who quietly labored to keep me on task until completion. To all of you, my humble thanks.

Introduction

Prayer in Jewish and Christian theology is simply the activity of faith. Pollsters tell us that more than 90 percent of Americans pray regularly, yet most of us regard prayer as a very personal and somewhat individual experience. By contrast, we at Bellarmine Prep have a tradition of starting class with a community prayer that respects both the social and individual character of each person. *Prayers for the Classroom* is meant to be a practical instrument that safeguards the individuality of the person praying, while it admits that our religious tradition encourages us to pray as a community. Easily we discover this opportunity to pray together in a number of such places as: our church, our home, our place of recreation, on a mountain, in a boat, but most of all this book focuses on our prayer in the classroom.

This format of *Prayers for the Classroom* is designed to help the busy teacher. Generally, there are about 180 days of school from September to June. For the sake of simplicity, this book is divided into the months of the school year from September 1 to June 1, with each month receiving the practical division of four weeks with five prayers for each week.

In December four weeks of prayers are provided with several prayers pertaining to the Christmas theme in the third and fourth week of the schedule. In November, Thanksgiving prayers are presented. In February and March, Lenten prayers are provided, and in April, following the general pattern of the liturgical season, some Resurrection themes are presented. In May, a few Pentecost prayers are given. Spring and fall each hold their own poetic and mystical spirit that this collection hopes to capture.

Obviously, the variety of these selections allows a teacher or student to choose a prayer at random depending on the desired theme. The index serves to meet this desire. I have sought a certain convenience of order, keeping in mind that too much order may disallow the Holy Spirit to touch us in yet spiritually unplanned ways.

Philip A. Verhalen

Suggested Use of This Book

At Bellarmine Preparatory School in Tacoma, Washington, we begin each class with a prayer. Because our religion department seeks among its goals an academic awareness of our Judeo-Christian traditions, we contrast the cerebral features of our class program with the specific goal of helping the students become comfortable with daily prayer.

As class begins, normally, I find myself involved with "nuts and bolts" chores of taking roll, signing permission slips, collecting assignments, etc. I always have soft classical music playing in the background so the transition from the last academic class such as mathematics or science to our religion class finds a buffer of ease. Basically, we as teachers acknowledge the plight of our students enduring the taxing daily schedule of classes. Before we begin our class, I seek out another aid to prayer—silence. If the students are unusually restless, or distracted by some unforeseen event immediately before class, we talk together about our distraction. Thus, we can more reasonably put the distraction aside and start our prayer.

If we cannot become tranquil and serene as a class, I engage the students in a few breathing exercises taken from a manual on centering prayer. The goal always is to achieve a proper atmosphere for prayer, since the classroom and the schedule are not of themselves conducive to prayer.

Finally, I, or one of the students assigned, open up this book of prayers and read the introduction to the prayer selected for the day. By now I have softened the music to make the sounds almost inaudible. After the introduction the reader pauses ever so briefly before slowly beginning the prayer of the day. When the prayer is completed, we pause again for a few seconds or minutes depending on the spirit of the class and the work of the Spirit in the class. Incidentally, all this time the lights are turned off and outside distractions are turned away by closed doors and closed windows.

When I, the teacher, believe the time of our prayer is completed, I turn on the lights, open the door and windows, and begin the class. Generally the entire experience takes three to five minutes.

1. September Prayers

Refreshed Beginnings

Morning Offering

This prayer comes from St. Ignatius of Loyola, founder of the Society of Jesus, the Jesuits. It is a prayer of offering based in gratitude coming from the depths of the heart. Whatever I want to give to God as a gift has already been given to me by him. But if the Lord continues to entrust these gifts to me, I will develop them for his service.

Take, Lord, and receive my entire liberty
—my memory, my understanding, my entire will.
All that I am and all that I have, You have given to me.
These are my greatest gifts, and now I offer them
    back to you.
Give me only Your love and Your grace.
With these I will be rich enough, and I will ask for
    nothing more.

Amen.

Being Alone

At times we all wish to be alone. We seek out a quiet place, peaceful and suitable for reflection. Our human condition yearns for quiet as part of our daily life. With Rabbi Nachman we pray now for the gift of a daily quiet experience.

Grant me the ability to be alone.
May it be my custom to go outdoors each day
among the trees and grasses,
among all growing things
and there may I be alone,
and enter into prayer
to talk with the one
that I belong to.

Rabbi Nachman of Bratzlaw

Sanctity of Life

Life is sacred! A truism beaten and burnt by the forces of a violent angry culture. Jo Poore calls us to meditate anew on life and creation coming from the hand of God.

> **Mother, Father, God, Universal Power**
> **Remind us daily of the sanctity of all life**
>
> **Touch our hearts with the glorious oneness of all**
> **creation,**
> **As we strive to respect all the living beings on this**
> **planet.**
>
> **Penetrate our souls with the beauty of this earth,**
> **As we attune ourselves to the rhythm and flow of**
> **the seasons.**
>
> **Awaken our minds with the knowledge to achieve**
> **a world in perfect harmony**
> **And grant us the wisdom to realize that we can**
> **have heaven on earth.**

Jo Poore
Earth Prayers

Jesus the Vine, We the Branches

To be "well-connected" in the spiritual life is to be close to Christ. The image of a vine and its branches draws our attention to the closeness that is essential for the growth of our spiritual life. The Gospel of John says:

> "I am the vine, and my Father is the vinegrower. He removes every branch in me that bears no fruit. Every branch that bears fruit he prunes to make it bear more fruit. You have already been cleansed by the word that I have spoken to you. Abide in me as I abide in you. Just as the branch cannot bear fruit by itself unless it abides in the vine, neither can you unless you abide in me. I am the vine, you are the branches. Those who abide in me and I in them bear much fruit, because apart from me you can do nothing. Whoever does not abide in me is thrown away like a branch and withers; such branches are gathered, thrown into the fire, and burned. If you abide in me, and my words abide in you, ask for whatever you wish, and it will be done for you."
>
> *John 15:1-7*

A Prayer for Wisdom

Here is another famous essay by our good friend Anonymous in
a prayer of petition.

> I asked for health,
> that I might do greater things:
> I was given infirmity,
> that I might do better things. . . .
> I asked for riches,
> that I might be happy:
> I was given poverty,
> that I might be wise . . .
> I asked for power,
> that I might have the praise of other persons:
> I was given weakness,
> that I might feel the need of God. . . .
> I asked for all things,
> that I might enjoy life:
> I was given life,
> that I might enjoy all things . . .
> I got nothing I asked for,
> but everything I hope for.
> Almost despite myself,
> my unspoken prayers were answered,
> I am among all persons most richly blessed.

Anonymous

God, Our Care Giver,
Knows Our Every Thought

Psalm 139 trades on the relationship between God our creator and us, God's creatures. Each section reveals how close God is to us and our every thought and deed. Not only do we realize we cannot escape God, we learn we do not want to escape the caring presence of God.

O LORD, you have searched me and known me.
You know when I sit down and when I rise up;
    you discern my thoughts from far away.
You search out my path and my lying down,
    and are acquainted with all my ways.
Even before a word is on my tongue,
    O LORD, you know it completely.
You hem me in, behind and before,
    and lay your hand upon me.
Such knowledge is too wonderful for me;
    it is so high that I cannot attain it.
Where can I go from your spirit?
    Or where can I flee from your presence?
If I ascend to heaven, you are there;
    if I make my bed in Sheol, you are there.
If I take the wings of the morning
    and settle at the farthest limits of the sea,
even there your hand shall lead me,
    and your right hand shall hold me fast.
If I say, "Surely the darkness shall cover me,
    and the light around me become night,"
Even the darkness is not dark to you;
    the night is as bright as the day,
    for darkness is as light to you.

PRAYER ONE

For it was you who formed my inward parts;
   you knit me together in my mother's womb.
I praise you, for I am fearfully and wonderfully
      made.
   Wonderful are all your works;
that I know very well.
   My frame was not hidden from you,
when I was being made in secret,
   intricately woven in the depths of the earth.
Your eyes beheld my unformed substance.
In your book were written
   all the days that were formed for me,
   when none of them as yet existed.
How weighty to me are your thoughts, O God!
   How vast is the sum of them!
I try to count them—they are more than the sand;
Search me, O God, and know my heart:
   test me and know my thoughts.
See if there is any wicked way in me,
   and lead me in the way everlasting.

Psalm 139:1-18, 23, 24

Footprints

A collection of prayers would not be complete without the famous prayer called "Footprints."

One night a man had a dream. He dreamed he was walking along the beach with the Lord. Across the sky flashed the scenes from his life. For each scene, he noticed two sets of footprints in the sand: one belonging to him, and the other to the Lord.

When the last scene of his life flashed before him, he looked back at the footprints in the sand. He noticed that at many times along the path of his life there was only one set of footprints. He also noticed that it happened at the very lowest and saddest times in his life.

This really bothered him and he questioned the Lord about it. "Lord, you said that once I decided to follow you, you'd walk with me all the way. But I have noticed that during the most troublesome times of my life, there is only one set of footprints. I don't understand why when I needed you most you would leave me."

The Lord replied, "My precious, precious child, I love you and would never leave you. During your times of trial and suffering, when you see only one set of footprints, it was then that I carried you."

Anonymous

Studies

So often our minds are preoccupied with coming tests or exams. If we can bring a prayerful heart to this flurry of mental worry, we might better place the role of studies in our total life.

Lord, give me the grace to do my best in all my studies.
Through all the things I learn,
may I come to know and to love you better.
Rather than my own profit,
may your honor and glory and the service of others
be the motive that inspires me.
Give me a love of the truth,
perseverance in difficulties,
modesty in success and cheerfulness in failure.

What Are Years?

Marianne Moore's understanding of the mystery of mortality
supports our questioning heart in a fast-paced world.

> What is our innocence, what
>   is our guilt? All are
>   naked, none is safe. And whence
> is courage: the unanswered question,
> the resolute doubt—
> dumbly calling, deadly listening—that
> in misfortune, even death,
>   encourages other
>   and in its defeat, stirs
>
>   the soul to be strong? He
> sees deep and is glad, who
>   accedes to mortality
> and in his imprisonment, rises
> upon himself as
> the sea in a chasm, struggling to be
> free and unable to be,
>   in its surrendering
>   finds its continuing.
>
>   So he who strongly feels,
> behaves. The very bird,
>   grown taller as he sings, steels
> his form straight up. Though he is captive,
> his mighty singing
> says, satisfaction is a lowly
> thing, how pure a thing is joy.
>   This is mortality,
>   this is eternity.

Faith

Faith is our response to the revelation of God. How well the Jews sensed their closeness to God; how appreciative they were of their faith!

Now faith is the assurance of things hoped for, the conviction of things not seen. Indeed, by faith our ancestors received approval. By faith we understand that the worlds were prepared by the word of God, so that what is seen was made from things that are not visible. . . .

By faith Abraham obeyed when he was called to set out for a place that he was to receive as an inheritance; and he set out, not knowing where he was going. By faith he stayed for a time in the land he had been promised, as in a foreign land, living in tents, as did Isaac and Jacob, who were heirs with him of the same promise. For he looked forward to the city that has foundations, whose architect and builder is God.

Hebrews 11:1-3, 8-10

Possessions

The words "charity," and "poverty" flow from the Gospels, urging us to attitudes and actions. But I ponder now, what might I possess that possesses me? What can I let go and not be upset? Ideally, we should be able to let go of everything, lest the meaning of life escape us.

A prayer that comes to me now arises from André Gide, who says:

"Complete possession is proved only by giving. All you are unable to give possesses you."

Random Acts of Kindness

PRAYER TWO

Power, Greed, and Corruption

The ancients tell the story of a great-hearted soul who ran through the city streets crying, "Power, greed, and corruption. Power, greed, and corruption." For a time, at least, the attentions of the people were riveted on this single-minded, open-hearted person for whom all of life had become focused on one great question. But then, eventually, everyone went back to work, some only slightly hearing, others clearly annoyed. However, the cries continued: "Power, greed, and corruption. Power, greed, and corruption."

One day a child stepped in front of the wailing figure. "Elder," said the child, "don't you realize that no one is listening to you?" "Of course I do, my child," the Elder answered. "Then why do you shout?" the child inquired as if in disbelief. "If nothing is changing, your efforts are useless." "Ah, dear child, these efforts are never useless," said the Elder. "You see, I do not shout only in order to change the people, I shout so that they cannot change me."

Anonymous

The Mountains Grow Unnoticed

Somewhat akin to the process of a mountain growing, we think of our spiritual life as limited by a very slow almost imperceptible growth. As if a reminder, Emily Dickinson tells us how slowly the mountains grow.

> **The mountains grow unnoticed,**
> **Their purple figures rise**
> **Without attempt, exhaustion,**
> **Assistance or applause.**
>
> **In their eternal faces**
> **The sun with broad delight**
> **Looks long—and last—and golden,**
> **For fellowship at night.**

Then one day there is an earthquake, and the mountains grow instantly, if not imperceptibly, several inches or feet. The constant splendor of the mountain shows itself nonetheless in its daily living. Likewise, our human lives offer many opportunities to show us that we too do not live vain, empty lives, admitting no measure of growth. Emily Dickinson encourages us in another poem to recognize the rich opportunities for growth in our routine lives.

> **If I can stop one heart from breaking**
> **I shall not live in vain:**
> **If I can ease one life the aching,**
> **Or cool one pain,**
> **Or help one fainting robin**
> **Unto his nest again,**
> **I shall not live in vain.**

Emily Dickinson (1830–1886)

Truth

The Greek philosophers held to three chief values: goodness, truth, and beauty. With varying degrees of success, we seek out those values and their variations in time and circumstance. A rather simple but poignant reflection in the value of truth comes to us from Coventry Patmore. He saw the lie as a most disruptive diabolical impediment to full social living. He cautions us against seeing any long term benefits in lying:

Here, in this little bay,
Full of tumultuous life and great repose,
Where, twice a day,
The purposeless, glad ocean comes and goes,
Under high cliffs, and far from the huge town,
I sit me down.
For want of me the world's course will not fail;
When all its work is done, the lie shall rot.
The truth is great, and shall prevail,
When none cares whether it prevail or not.

Coventry Patmore (1823–1896)

Morning Prayer

Beneath my clock in the classroom I have the prayer from Psalm 118: "This is the day that the Lord has made, Let us rejoice and be glad in it."

Maurice Boyd suggests the following prayer as a fitting morning prayer. We recall that New Testament scholars tell us that we may look at each new day as a resurrection, having put to rest the cares and trials of the day before. In the spirit of Christ's resurrection, we offer the following:

"Eternal God, this new day is the gift of your love; teach us to rejoice and be glad in it. If the day should prove difficult, grant us courage, cheerfulness and a quick mind. Teach us to remember that each day has troubles enough of its own, so that we don't try to carry tomorrow's burdens with today's strength. When we are threatened by uncertainties, remind us that your loving-kindness is there to meet us at every corner. Help us to keep a good opinion of ourselves, and bring us safely through nightfall."

Amen.

R. Maurice Boyd

Mystical Body of Christ

In the middle of World War II, Pope Pius XII decided to review a basic idea of our faith, namely, that we are all members of one body called the Mystical Body. He published an encyclical, by that name. In this letter he highlighted the principle that all of us are members, one to another, of one body. What follows is one passage of Paul describing quite prayerfully the same topic.

For just as the body is one and has many members, and all the members of the body, though many, are one body, so it is with Christ. For in the one Spirit we were all baptized into one body—Jews or Greeks, slaves or free—and we were all made to drink of one Spirit.

Indeed, the body does not consist of one member but of many. If the foot would say, "Because I am not a hand, I do not belong to the body," that would not make it any less a part of the body. And if the ear would say, "Because I am not an eye, I do not belong to the body," that would not make it any less a part of the body. If the whole body were an eye, where would the hearing be? If the whole body were hearing, where would the sense of smell be? But as it is, God arranged the members in the body, each one of them, as he chose. If all were a single member, where would the body be? As it is, there are many members, yet one body.

1 Corinthians 12:12-20

Kindness at Random

Maya Angelou has often spoken of surviving a childhood full of terror and violence. Creative artists over the years consoled her, but always at a distance and not knowing how much they did for her. Eventually, Maya publicly thanked these creative souls for their "random acts of kindness."

Strangely enough those words of Maya touched another person and prompted a work by yet another group of creative artists, who put a book together called *Random Acts of Kindness*. It is a warm, gentle, and at times overwhelming work. It's message is simple: "Be kind; you can make a difference." The authors suggest that random, and the operative word is random, acts of kindness are "those little sweet or grand lovely things we do for no reason except that, momentarily, the best of our humanity has sprung exquisitely, into full bloom." The acts are not what life requires of us, but what is best in us.

Among the suggestions are:

- **Put coins in a parking meter of a stranger's car because you see the red "expired" marker signalling to a meter maid, or**

- **Laugh out loud often, and share your smile generously**

How easily these random acts of kindness show us that we are praying!

PRAYER THREE

God, the Unknown

As long as we live, we run the danger of becoming discouraged in our faith. We need support and reinforcement that we do not believe in vain, and that there is a true God guiding us no matter how unknowable this God is. Anthony de Mello gives us a most pleasant story about a bird compelled to sing. He says:

The disciples were full of questions about God.

Said the Master, "God is the Unknown and the Unknowable. Every statement made about Him, every answer to your questions, is a distortion of the Truth."

The disciples were bewildered. "Then why do you speak about Him at all?"

"Why does the bird sing?" said the Master.

A bird does not sing because he has a statement. He sings because he has a song.

The words of the Scholar are to be understood. The words of the Master are not to be understood. They are to be listened to as one listens to the wind in the trees and the sound of the river and the song of the bird. They will awaken something within the heart that is beyond all knowledge.

The Song of the Bird

Jesus—Way, Truth, Life

The "Good News" tells us that Jesus is "the way, the truth, and the life." These words weave in and out of a prose of various meanings. Yet, in time, the words stand out on their own, and we assess how our faith acknowledges the power of these words describing Jesus. George Herbert prays:

> **Come, my Way, my Truth, my Life:**
> **Such a Way as gives us breath:**
> **Such a Truth as ends all strife:**
> **Such a Life as killeth death.**
>
> **Come, my Light, my Feast, my Strength:**
> **Such a Light, as shows a feast:**
> **Such a Feast, as mends in length:**
> **Such a Strength, as makes his guest.**
>
> **Come, my Joy, my Love, my Heart:**
> **Such a Joy, as none can move:**
> **Such a Love, as none can part:**
> **Such a Heart, as joys in love.**

George Herbert (1593–1633)

Adoration

To pray to God is a paradox. We need to stretch to rise to the endeavor, but we need to be relaxed to assimilate the richness of the mystery. Sister Ruth acknowledges the paradox in her prayer of adoration.

O God, let me rise to the edges of time and
  open my life to your eternity;
 let me run to the edges of space and
  gaze into your immensity;
 let me climb through the barriers of sound
  and pass into your silence;
And then, in stillness and silence
 let me adore You,
  Who are Life—Light—Love—
  without beginning and without end,
 the Source—the Sustainer—the Restorer—
  the Purifier—of all that is;
 the Lover who has bound earth to heaven
  by the beams of a cross;
 the Healer who has renewed a dying race
  by the blood of a chalice;
 the God who has taken man into your glory
  by the wounds of sacrifice;
God . . . God . . . God . . . Blessed be God
 Let me adore you.

Oxford Book of Prayer

2. October Prayers

*The Fun of Fall Leaves
and Golden Sunsets
Before the Harvest Moon*

Effective Prayer

According to surveys conducted in the United States over the last decades, Americans consistently believe in the power of prayer. What all of us wonder about is how effective our prayer really is. In the Sermon on the Mount, Matthew consoles us with the words of Jesus concerning prayer.

"Ask, and it will be given you; search, and you will find; knock, and the door will be opened for you. For everyone who asks receives, and everyone who searches finds, and for everyone who knocks, the door will be opened. Is there anyone among you who, if your child asks for bread, will give a stone? If the child asks for a fish, will give a snake? If you then, who are evil, know how to give good gifts to your children, how much more will your Father in heaven give good things to those who ask him!

Matthew 7:7-11

Prayer of St. Francis

The Prayer of St. Francis of Assisi focuses on the role of service. Francis reminds us that our relation to God and to our fellow human beings is preeminently one of service.

Giving is what life is all about according to this remarkable prayer of the founder of Franciscan spirituality. We celebrate his feast on October 4.

> **Lord, make me an instrument of your peace.**
> **Where there is hatred, let me sow love,**
> **Where there is injury, pardon;**
> **Where there is doubt, faith;**
> **Where there is despair, hope;**
> **Where there is darkness, light;**
> **Where there is sadness, joy;**
> **O divine Master, Grant that I may not so much seek**
> **To be consoled, as to console,**
> **To be understood, as to understand**
> **To be loved, as to love,**
> **For it is in giving that we receive;**
> **It is in pardoning that we are pardoned;**
> **It is in dying that we are born to eternal life.**

St. Francis of Assisi (1181–1226)

Creation

The earth created by God is sacred. Hildegard of Bingen called us to recall prayerfully the privilege of earth dwelling and the pain of misusing our planet.

**The high,
the low
all of creation,
God gives to humankind to use. If this privilege is
    misused,
God's justice permits creation to punish humanity.**

Hildegard of Bingen

The Brevity of Life

Think of a long rich life of accomplishment; then turn your thoughts to the long robust evolutionary changes on this planet over billions of years. By comparison our life on earth is a very brief life. Ernest Dowson celebrates this fact:

They are not long, the weeping and the laughter,
　　Love and desire and hate;
I think they have no portion in us after
　　We pass the gate.

They are not long, the days of wine and roses;
　　Out of a misty dream
Our path emerges for awhile, then closes
　　Within a dream.

Ernest Dowson (1867–1900)
From Vitae Summa Brevis Spem Nos Vetat
Incohare Longham

Strength for the Weary

As youth we feel we have unlimited energy. Yet, we too grow tired and seek out a time of rest. Isaiah points out that God renews our strength and often gives us strength and endurance that surprises us!

Have you not known? Have you not heard?
The Lord is the everlasting God,
the Creator of the ends of the earth.
He does not faint or grow weary;
his understanding is unsearchable.
He gives power to the faint,
and strengthens the powerless.
Even youths will faint and be weary,
and the young will fall exhausted;
but those who wait for the Lord shall
renew their strength,
they shall mount up with wings like eagles,
they shall run and not be weary,
they shall walk and not faint.

Isaiah 40:28-31

Blessings for Creation

The Chinook Psalter reads much like the psalms of the Hebrew Psalter. The two quite "up beat" prayer books urge us to offer blessings in praise of God and her creative powers.

Blessing of galaxies, blessing of stars:
  Great stars, small stars, red stars, blue ones.
Blessing of nebula, blessing of supernova,
  Planets, satellites, asteroids, comets.

Blessing of our sun and moon, blessing of our earth;
  Oceans, rivers, continents, mountain ranges
Blessing of wind and cloud, blessing of rain;
  Fog bank, snowdrift, lightning and thunder.

Bless the wisdom of the holy one above us.
Bless the truth of the holy one beneath us.
Bless the love of the holy one within us.

Blessing of green plants, blessing of forests:
  Cedar, douglas fir, swordfern, salal bush
Blessing of fish and birds, blessing of mammals:
  Salmon, eagle, cougar and mountain goat.

May all humankind likewise offer blessing:
  Old woman, young woman, wise men and foolish
Blessing of youthfulness, blessing of children
  Big boys, little boys, big girls and little ones.

Bless the wisdom of the holy one above us.
Bless the truth of the holy one beneath us.
Bless the love of the holy one within us.

Chinook Psalter
Earth Prayers

PRAYER TWO

The Inmost Fear

One of the most frequently used phrases in Our Lord's public preaching and teaching was "Do not fear." He explains that we need not fear because God is with us. David Hassel poetically moves us through the question of fear as a solution we can all recognize.

> **Why do I fear?**
> **God is here, deep within—**
> **covering nakedness,**
> **mothering boldness,**
> **sustaining exuberance,**
> **restraining insolence,**
> **stirring insight,**
> **firing lovelight,**
> **fulfilling hollowness,**
> **instilling hallowedness**
> **of lung, limb, and life**
> **with tongued fire and crossed strife—**
> **through Christ's indwelling,**
> **outwelling, sorrow-quelling,**
> **joy-swelling victory—**
> **warm love straining**
> **to be heard, to be loved,**
> **yet quiet as a craning ear in silent expectation,**
> **as simple and lonely as a man's sigh,**
> **as rich and crowded as God's sea**
> **in which I swim to eternity**
> **alone in crowded company—**
> **I, mere glint of God's light,**
> **a mere hint of his might,**
> **yet having the mint of his Son on my heart:**

a cross-sweeping to God's glorying
and a love flaming with God's worrying—
Christ about me,
in me,
with me,
today the darkening fierce joy of God's sorrow
and then the tranquil swift dawn of God's
   tomorrow.
Why, then, do I fear?
God is here,
   deep within, forever:
   Life grandly vibrant,
   Love scandalously flagrant,
   yet heart quietly homing
   and Lord wisely lording.
   But, then,—why do I fear?
   . . . fear . . . fear . . . fear . . .

David J. Hassel, S.J.

God, the Creator

In Psalm 104 the author prays that the creator may "find joy in what he creates." You and I move toward God as creatures, but also as co-creators. God empowers us to work in this world of nature to create new ideas, new products, even new life. Finally, to share with God in the joy of creating new human life is the greatest gift of a mother or father.

> Bless the LORD, O my soul.
>> O LORD, my God, you are very great.
> You are clothed with honor and majesty,
>> wrapped in light as with a garment.
> You stretch out the heavens like a tent,
>> you set the beams of your chambers
>>> on the waters,
> you make the clouds your chariot,
>> you ride on the wings of the wind,
> you make the winds your messengers,
>> fire and flame your ministers.
>
> You have made the moon to mark the seasons;
>> the sun knows its time for setting.
> You make the darkness, and it is night,
>> when all the animals of the forest come
>>> creeping out.
> The young lions roar for their prey,
>> seeking their food from God.
> When the sun rises, they withdraw
>> and lie down in their dens.
> People go out to their work
>> and to their labor until the evening.

PRAYER THREE

O LORD, how manifold are your works!
    In wisdom you have made them all;
    the earth is full of your creatures.
Yonder is the sea, great and wide,
    creeping things innumerable are there,
    living things both small and great.

May the glory of the LORD endure forever;
    may the LORD rejoice in his works—
who looks on the earth and it trembles,
    who touches the mountains and they smoke.
I will sing to the LORD as long as I live;
    I will sing praise to my God while I have being.
May my meditation be pleasing to him,
    for I rejoice in the LORD.

Psalm 104:1-4, 19-25, 31-34

The Prayer of the Tortoise

Everyone of us is handicapped in some way. We adjust to our handicap, or try to eliminate the handicap, depending on our circumstances. The subtle handicaps of our life—social, emotional, or even intellectual keep us humble. In our faith life we place our handicap in God's hands. One way to live effectively with our handicaps is to imagine how an animal might pray to God, given its distinct handicap. Below is a prayer written by Carmen De Gasztold in the name of a tortoise:

> **A little patience.**
> **O God,**
> **I am coming.**
> **One must take nature as she is!**
> **It was not I who made her!**
> **I do not mean to criticize**
> **this house on my back—**
> **it has its points—**
> **but You must admit, Lord,**
> **it is heavy to carry!**
> **Still,**
> **let us hope that this double enclosure,**
> **my shell and my heart,**
> **will never be quite shut to You.**
>
> **Amen.**

Incarnation of Christ in the World

For years before the Second Vatican Council, the Roman Catholic liturgy ended with a "Last Gospel" taken from the opening verses of John's Gospel. In these fourteen verses John tells of the cosmic mystery of God choosing to become a human person.

In the beginning was the Word, and the Word was with God, and the Word was God. He was in the beginning with God. All things came into being through him, and without him not one thing came into being. What has come into being in him was life, and the life was the light of all people. The light shines in darkness, and the darkness did not overcome it.

There was a man sent from God, whose name was John. He came as a witness to testify to the light, so that all might believe through him. He himself was not the light, but he came to testify to the light. The true light, which enlightens everyone, was coming into the world.

He was in the world, and the world came into being through him; yet the world did not know him. He came to what was his own, and his own people did not accept him. But to all who received him, who believed in his name, he gave power to become children of God, who were born, not of blood or of the will of the flesh or of the will of man; but of God.

And the Word became flesh and lived among us, and we have seen his glory, the glory as of a father's only son, full of grace and truth.

John 1:1-14

PRAYER ONE

Prayer of Thanks

In our thoughts of thanksgiving, we easily omit various men and women, boys and girls who interact in our lives but escape our notice as valuable to our growth in faith. The following prayer expands our thoughts to include our contacts with the wide community meeting us on a daily basis.

We thank you, O God, for the people who enrich our lives:

- **for those who are always willing to be a sounding board;**
- **for friends who accept us for what we are;**
- **for competitors who bring out the best in us;**
- **for critics who, while irritating us, challenge us to prove them wrong;**
- **for counselors, teachers, and pastors who share good advice;**
- **for all those who love us and care for us;**
- **for those who set an example worthy to be followed;**
- **for those whose moral sensitivity pricks our conscience and challenges our self-indulgence.**

PRAYER TWO

Morning Has Broken

Here is another morning prayer that has been set to music and greets the freshness of each day.

Morning has broken, like the first morning. Blackbird has spoken, like the first bird. Praise for the singing, praise for the morning, praise for them springing, fresh from the word.

Sweet the rains new fall, sunlit from heaven. Like the first dewfall on the first grass. Praise for the sweetness of the wet garden, sprung in completeness where his feet pass.

Mine is the sunlight, mine is the morning, born of the one light, Eden saw play. Praise with elation, praise every morning, God's recreation of the new day.

From "The Children's Bells"

God in Nature

When a person tells me of her struggle with a basic understanding of God, I am reminded how I used to go to philosophers and theologians to assist me in providing background for a reasonable discussion about the nature of God. Of late, I likewise look in other directions. Walt Whitman is one poet I examine. He clearly tells me of his ease and serenity in recognizing God in nature. Although we do not understand all the scientific elements of nature, we may nonetheless see in nature a relationship to God that almost indicates the belonging qualities of life linked to each living thing.

> **A child said, What is the grass? Fetching it to me**
>   **with full hands;**
> **How could I answer the child? I do not know what**
>   **is any more than he.**
> **I guess it must be the flag of my disposition, out of**
>   **hopeful green stuff woven.**
> **Or I guess it is the handkerchief of the Lord,**
> **A scented gift and remembrancer designedly dropt,**
> **Bearing the owner's name someway in the corner,**
>   **that we may see and remark, and say Whose?**

From "Song of Myself"
Walt Whitman (1819–1892)

Love

The abiding classic comment on the mystery of love flows from the pen of St. Paul. He touches all of us, but as we grow older he touches us more forcefully each time we read this stirring passage. Paul leads us through all of our false dreams and ambitions to the point of seeing the ultimate value of love.

If I speak in the tongues of mortals and of angels, but do not have love, I am a noisy gong or a clanging cymbal. And if I have prophetic powers, and understand all mysteries and all knowledge, and I have all faith, so as to remove mountains, but do not have love, I am nothing. If I give away all my possessions, and if I hand over my body so that I may boast, but do not have love, I gain nothing.

Love is patient; love is kind; love is not envious or boastful or arrogant or rude. It does not insist on its own way; it is not irritable or resentful; it does not rejoice in wrongdoing, but rejoices in the truth. It bears all things, believes all things, hopes all things, endures all things.

Love never ends. But as for prophecies, they will come to an end; as for tongues, they will cease; as for knowledge, it will come to an end. For we know only in part, and we prophesy only in part; but when the complete comes, the partial will come to an end. When I was a child, I spoke like a child, I thought like a child, I reasoned like a child; when I became an adult, I put an end to childish ways. For now we see in a mirror, dimly, but then we will see face to face. Now I know only in part; then I will know fully, even as I have been fully known. And now faith, hope, and love abide, these three; and the greatest of these is love.

1 Corinthians 13:1-13

God's Will

The mystery of doing God's will is one of the chief mysteries of the spiritual life. Upon reaching the age of free decisions, we wrestle with the problem of making the correct decision personally, correct in the sense that God would approve it.

In the Letter of James, we have a brief passage where this Christian phrase "God willing" originated. As we read this passage from an early Christian speech of exhortation, we can ask once again: "Am I doing God's Will?"

> **Come now, you who say, "Today or tomorrow we will go to such and such a town and spend a year there, doing business and making money." Yet you do not even know what tomorrow will bring. What is your life? For you are a mist that appears for a little while, and then vanishes. Instead you ought to say, "If the Lord wishes, we will live and do this or that."**

James 4:13-15

And God Said "No"

When we pray to God with special requests we sometimes discover that the answer God gives to our prayers is "no"! To move past a simple "no" of God can be a significant breakthrough in our often delicately balanced spiritual lives. What follows is a prayer that steadily grows to accept the "no" of God, and puzzles over the idea that we may be asking not only for the wrong things, but also for more frivolous things than God wishes us to seek:

> I asked God to take away my pride,
> And God said, "No."
> He said it was not his to take away
> but for me to give up.
> I asked God to make my handicapped
> child whole,
> And God said, "No."
> He said her spirit was whole, her
> body was only temporary.
> I asked God to grant me patience,
> And God said, "No."
> He said that patience is a byproduct
> of tribulation, it isn't granted,
> it's earned.
> I asked God to give me happiness,
> And God said, "No."
> He said he gives blessing, happiness
> is up to me.
> I asked God to spare me pain,
> And God said, "No."
> He said "suffering draws you apart
> from worldly cares and brings
> you closer to me."

PRAYER ONE

I asked God to make my spirit grow,
And God said, "No."
He said I must grow on my own, but
he will prune me to make me
fruitful.
I asked God if he loved me,
And God said, "Yes."
He gave me his only son, who died
for me, and I will be in heaven
someday because I believe.
I asked God to help me love others
as much as he loved me,
And God said,
"Ah, finally, you have the idea."

Anonymous

PRAYER TWO

A Fitting Requiem

In the aftermath of the 1987 shuttle tragedy, a sonnet written by a nineteen-year-old American pilot killed during World War II was cited by President Reagan to evoke the courage and calling of the astronauts. "High Flight," by John Gillespie Magee, Jr., is a fitting requiem for the Challenger Seven:

Oh, I have slipped the surly bonds of earth,
And danced the skies on laughter-silvered wings;
Sunward I've climbed and joined the tumbling
   mirth
Of sun-split clouds—and done a hundred things
You have not dreamed of; wheeled and soared and
   swung
High in the sunlit silence. Hov'ring there,
I've chased the shouting wind along and flung
My eager craft through footless halls of air.
Up, up the long, delirious, burning blue
I've topped the wind-swept heights with easy
   grace.
Where never lark, or even eagle, flew;
And, while with silent, lifting mind I've trod
The high, untrespassed sanctity of space,
Put out my hand, and touched the face of God.

Monkey Salvation for a Fish

An entertainer needs an audience; a scholar needs solitude. A runner needs space; a tennis player needs but a small court. We all grow to learn the best environment for our species and personality. Anthony de Mello gives us a story to support our awareness of these unique differences in our human lives.

"What on earth are you doing?" said I to the monkey when I saw him lift a fish out of the water and place it on the branch of a tree.

"I am saving it from drowning," was the reply.

One man's meat is another man's poison.

The sun that gives sight to the eagle blinds the owl.

The Road Not Taken

Thoreau said that we must be true to ourselves. I add that we listen to ourselves as we cooperate with God's graces to hear what we are truly thinking. Thoreau comments: "If a man does not keep pace with his companions, perhaps it is because he hears a different drummer. Let him step to the music which he hears, however measured and far away."

In another way Robert Frost expands on the same idea in "The Road Not Taken."

> Two roads diverged in a yellow wood,
> And sorry I could not travel both
> And be one traveler, long I stood
>
> And looked down one as far as I could
> To where it bent in the undergrowth;
>
> Then took the other, as just as fair,
> And having perhaps the better claim,
> Because it was grassy and wanted wear;
> Though as for that the passing there
> Had worn them really about the same,
>
> And both that morning equally lay
> In leaves no step had trodden black.
> Oh, I kept the first for another day!
> Yet knowing how way leads on to way,
> I doubted if I should ever come back.
>
> I shall be telling this with a sigh
> Somewhere ages and ages hence:
> Two roads diverged in a wood, and I—
> I took the one less traveled by,
> And that has made all the difference.

Robert Frost

49

Evening Thoughts

John Henry Newman was both a scholar and a churchman. He identified with our prayers that needed to move beyond our daily needs, yet put our whole life into perspective.

> **May he support us all the day long,**
> **till shadows lengthen**
> **and the evening comes,**
> **and the busy world is hushed,**
> **and the fever of life is over,**
> **and our work is done!**
>
> **Then in his mercy may he grant us**
> **a safe lodging, a true rest, and**
> **peace at last.**
>
> **Amen.**

3. November Prayers

Saints
Sinners
All Holy Persons
Linked in Thanksgiving

Vessels of Clay

Down at the Seattle docks I have discovered that we ship so much of our goods in metal containers just short in size of a semi-trailer. This method of shipment appears to be the most efficient today. At the time of Christ, everything was shipped in large earthenware jars! When the goods arrived in port and were distributed, the merchants took the earthenware jars and broke them up and threw the shards in a pile. One such dramatic pile is found today near the Tiber River docks in Rome.

Paul tells us that spiritually we are vessels of clay. We carry the treasure of God's spirit in us, but we are merely earthenware jars that function in a certain way under God's plan. He says:

> **But we have this treasure in clay jars, so that it may be made clear that this extraordinary power belongs to God and does not come from us. We are afflicted in every way, but not crushed; perplexed, but not driven to despair; persecuted, but not forsaken; struck down, but not destroyed; always carrying in the body the death of Jesus, so that the life of Jesus may also be made visible in our bodies.**

> *2 Corinthians 4:7-10*

Letter from a Friend

Let me present this famous letter that some of you have already heard:

I just had to write to tell you how much I love you and care for you. Yesterday, I saw you walking and laughing with your friends; I hoped that soon you'd want me to walk along with you, too. So, I painted you a sunset to close your day and whispered a cool breeze to refresh you. I waited— you never called—I just kept on loving you.

As I watched you fall asleep last night, I wanted so much to touch you. I spilled moonlight onto your face—trickling down your cheeks as so many tears have. You didn't even think of me; I wanted so much to comfort you.

The next day I exploded a brilliant sunrise into glorious morning for you. But you woke up late and rushed off to work—you didn't even notice. My sky became cloudy and my tears were the rain.

I love you. Oh, if you'd only listen. I really love you. I try to say it in the quiet of the green meadow and in the blue sky. The wind whispers my love throughout the treetops and spills into the vibrant colors of all the flowers. I shout it to you in the thunder of the great waterfalls and compose love songs of birds to sing for you. I warm you with the clothing of my sunshine and perfume the air with nature's sweet scent. My love for you is deeper than any ocean and greater than any need in your heart. If you'd only realize how I care.

My Dad sends his love. I want you to meet him— He cares, too. Fathers are just that way. So, please call on me soon. No matter how long it takes. I'll wait—because I love you.

Your friend,
Jesus

Sabbath Rest

"Stop! I want to get off," we yell like children too tired to enjoy the merry-go-round. Numb and nearly senseless we stagger from the bedazzling circle of excitement only to realize we need to rest. As we grow older, we experience again and again the numbing, dizzying effects of the merry-go-round of life—careers, families, duties, pressures, over-achieving expectations leveled on us from all directions. We need to stop, to pause, to pray.

We who have lost our sense and our senses—our touch, our smell, our vision of who we are; we who frantically force and press all things, without rest for body or spirit, hurting our earth and injuring ourselves: we call a halt.

We want to rest. We need to rest and allow the earth to rest. We need to reflect and to rediscover the mystery that lives in us, that is the ground of every unique expression of life, the source of the fascination that calls all things to communion.

We declare a Sabbath, a space of quiet: for simply being and letting be; for recovering the great, forgotten truths; for learning how to live again.

U.N. Environmental Sabbath Program
Earth Prayers

Promise of a New Covenant

I often wonder, how much does God try to move me to action? What motives does God plant in my heart? Does the spirit of God have any palpable effect on me? In time of great anxiety I can turn to chapter 31 of Jeremiah and recall how God moved the Jewish people as a community.

The days are surely coming, says the Lord, when I will make a new covenant with the house of Israel and the house of Judah. It will not be like the covenant that I made with their ancestors when I took them by the hand to bring them out of the land of Egypt—a covenant that they broke, though I was their husband, says the Lord. But this is the covenant that I will make with the house of Israel after those days, says the Lord: I will put my law within them, and I will write it on their hearts; and I will be their God, and they shall be my people. No longer shall they teach one another, or say to each other, "Know the Lord," for they shall all know me, from the least of them to the greatest, says the Lord; for I will forgive their iniquity, and remember their sin no more.

Jeremiah 31:31-34

Conformity and Non-Conformity in Our Spiritual Lives

Paul mixes his exhortation to worship God with a call to personal sacrifice of our lives and efforts, always in contrast with conformity to this world.

> **I appeal to you therefore, brothers and sisters, by the mercies of God, to present your bodies as a living sacrifice, holy and acceptable to God, which is your spiritual worship. Do not be conformed to this world, but be transformed by the renewing of your minds, so that you may discern what is the will of God—what is good and acceptable and perfect.**
>
> *Romans 12:1-2*

Class Distinction—Love of Neighbor

James tells the story of a religious person unwittingly making a distinction between a rich and a poor man when he meets them in the synagogue. James repeats the second great commandment and contrasts that to the sinful habit of making distinctions between persons.

My brothers and sisters, do you with your acts of favoritism really believe in our glorious Lord Jesus Christ? For if a person with gold rings and in fine clothes comes into your assembly, and if a poor person in dirty clothes also comes in, and if you take notice of the one wearing fine clothes and say, "Have a seat here, please," while to the one who is poor you say, "Stand there," or, "Sit at my feet," have you not made distinctions among yourselves, and become judges with evil thoughts? Listen, my beloved brothers and sisters. Has not God chosen the poor in the world to be rich in faith and to be heirs of the kingdom that he has promised to those who love him? But you have dishonored the poor. Is it not the rich who oppress you? Is it not they who drag you into court? Is it not they who blaspheme the excellent name that was invoked over you?

You do well if you really fulfill the royal law according to the scripture, "You shall love your neighbor as yourself."

James 1:1-8

Humility and Service

There is a connection between service and humility. We can only serve one another, in the spirit of Jesus' Last Supper, if we are humble. Paul encourages us to make hospitality and service our special care.

For by the grace given to me I say to everyone among you not to think of yourself more highly than you ought to think, but to think with sober judgment, each according to the measure of faith that God has assigned. For as in one body we have many members, and not all the members have the same function, so we, who are many, are one body in Christ, and individually we are members of one another. We have gifts that differ according to the grace given to us: prophecy, in proportion to faith; ministry, in ministering; the teacher, in teaching; the exhorter, in exhortation; the giver, in generosity; the leader, in diligence; the compassionate, in cheerfulness.

Let love be genuine; hate what is evil, hold fast to what is good; love one another with mutual affection; outdo one another in showing honor. Do not lag in zeal, be ardent in spirit, serve the Lord. Rejoice in hope, be patient in suffering, persevere in prayer. Contribute to the needs of the saints; extend hospitality to strangers.

Romans 12:3-13

The Solid Christian Life

Sitting quietly in a local restaurant, I realize that life has so much to appreciate. Each person we meet or merely see reminds us of the goodness of creation. Certainly there are problems rampant in our life, but how remarkable it is to see these people overcoming their problems and living a rather meaningful life despite its shortcomings and setbacks. Micah, the prophet, explained so simply what is the proper solid posture for Judeo-Christian living.

> **He has told you, O mortal, what is good:**
> **and what does the Lord require of you**
> **but to do justice, and to love kindness,**
> **and to walk humbly with your God?**

Micah 6:8

Trust in God

Leo Buscaglia consoles us by revealing that 90 percent of all our worries never come to pass. We are a worrisome people, but often because we are insecure. The psalmist in the following psalm prays for the tranquility of a child in her mother's arms. If we become childlike in our spirituality, we will find complete security in God and not in our mere ability to struggle for the limited security that this material world offers.

> O LORD, my heart is not lifted up,
> my eyes are not raised too high;
> I do not occupy myself with things
> too great and too marvelous for me.
> But I have calmed and quieted my soul,
> like a weaned child with its mother.

Psalm 131:1, 2

Being Blessed

Sometimes a contrast prayer is appropriate. We live in a world where East has already met West, where trade and commerce between the two are the norm, where sixteen Pacific Rim nations are in daily communication. To live thus allows for the wisdom of both cultures to penetrate our lives. Let us begin our prayer with the Beatitudes from the Sermon on the Mount:

Blessed Are the Poor in Spirit

Blessed are the poor in spirit, for theirs is the kingdom of heaven.

Blessed are those who mourn, for they will be comforted.

Blessed are the meek, for they will inherit the earth.

Blessed are those who hunger and thirst for righteousness, for they will be filled.

Blessed are the merciful, for they will receive mercy.

Blessed are the pure in heart, for they will see God.

Blessed are the peacemakers, for they will be called children of God.

Blessed are those who are persecuted for righteousness' sake, for theirs is the kingdom of heaven.

Matthew 5:3-10

The Song of Blessing

Now let us turn to a similar prayer from the culture of the East:

Not to serve the foolish, but to serve the wise,
To honor those worthy of honor—this is the highest
   blessing.

Much insight and education, self-control and
   pleasant speech,
And whatever word be well-spoken—this is the
   highest blessing.

Service to mother and father, the company of wife
   and child,
And peaceful pursuits—this is the highest blessing.

Almsgiving and righteousness, the company of
   kinsfolk,
Blameless works—this is the highest blessing.

To dwell in a pleasant land, with right desire in the
   heart,
To hear remembrance of good deeds—this is the
   highest blessing.

Reverence and humility, cheerfulness and gratitude,
Listening in due season to the Dhamma—this is the
   highest blessing.

Self-control and virtue, vision of the Noble Truths,
And winning to Nirvana—this is the highest
   blessing.

Beneath the stroke of life's changes, the mind that
   does not shake

But abides without grief or passion—this is the
highest blessing.

On every side invincible are they who do thus,
They come to salvation—theirs is the highest
blessing.

Sutta Nipata, 258, Pali Canon

The Toys

We hear the phrase "children of God" so often in our religious training that we lose all sense of its poetic potency. Coventry Patmore reintroduces us to our status as children beloved by a Father so understanding, so forgiving that we can completely rest all our concerns in his lap of love.

My little son, who looked from thoughtful eyes
And moved and spoke in quiet grown-up wise,
Having my law the seventh time disobeyed,
I struck him, and dismissed
With hard words and unkissed,
His mother, who was patient, being dead.
Then, fearing lest his grief should hinder sleep,
I visited his bed,

But found him slumbering deep,
With darkened eyelids, and their lashes yet
From his late sobbing wet.
And I, with moan,
Kissing away his tears, left others of my own;
For, on a table drawn beside his head,
He had put, within his reach,
A box of counters and a red-veined stone,
A piece of glass abraded by the beach,
And six or seven shells,
A bottle with bluebells,
And two French copper coins, ranged there with
  careful art,
To comfort his sad heart.

So when that night I prayed
To God, I wept, and said:

PRAYER ONE

"Ah, when at last we lie with tranced breath,
Not vexing Thee in death,
And Thou rememberest of what toys
We made our joys,
How weakly understood
Thy great commanded good.
Then, fatherly not less
Than I whom Thou has molded from the clay,
Thou'lt leave Thy wrath, and say,
'I will be sorry for their childishness.'"

Coventry Patmore (1823–1896)

Presence of God

Our busy routine often distracts us from being aware of our presence in the presence of God.

> You have, O God, created us to live in the present
> moment,
> but have also planted eternity in our hearts.
> You have created us as bodies and minds,
> but have also created us as living souls.
> You have given us the power of communication
> with others,
> but have also assured us that you hear our needs.
> Give us, we pray, a sensibility of your presence,
> and help us to experience life at its greatest.
>
> Amen.

The Truth Shop

Truth comes at a price. Often we become isolated or disturbed by the full force of truth. Anthony de Mello tells another story about truth.

I could hardly believe my eyes when I saw the name of the shop: THE TRUTH SHOP. They sold truth there.

The salesgirl was very polite: What type of truth did I wish to purchase, partial truth or whole truth? The whole truth, of course. No deceptions for me, no defenses, no rationalizations. I wanted my truth plain and clear and whole. She waved me on to another side of the store where the whole truth was sold.

The salesman there looked at me compassionately and pointed to the price tag. "The price is very high, sir," he said. "What is it?" I asked, determined to get the whole truth, no matter what it cost. "If you take this," he said, "you will pay for it by losing all repose for the rest of your life."

I walked sadly out of the store. I had thought I could have the whole truth at little cost. I am still not ready for Truth. I crave for peace and rest every now and then. I still need to deceive myself a little with my defenses and rationalizations. I still seek the shelter of my unquestioned beliefs.

The Song of the Bird

PRAYER FOUR

Thanksgiving

John Wesley, the Anglican priest who founded Methodism, offers the following eco-sensitive prayer of thanksgiving:

> **"Bless our hearts**
> **to hear in the**
> **breaking of bread**
> **the song of the universe."**

With the same sensitivity to our universe Tecumseh, the chief of the Shawnee nation, offers his prayer:

> **"When you arise in the morning,**
> **give thanks for the morning light,**
> **for your life and strength.**
> **Give thanks for your food**
> **and the joy of living.**
> **If you see no reason for giving thanks,**
> **the fault lies in yourself."**

Tecumseh (1768–1813)

This Thanksgiving Day

On this Thanksgiving Day as we specifically give thanks for all God's gifts and blessings, we should remember to give thanks and praise to the Lord our God. We are happy to do so not only on this glad day but always and everywhere.

Thankful may I ever be for everything that God bestows. Thankful for the joys and sorrows, for the blessings and the blows. Thankful for the wisdom gained through hardships and adversity. Thankful for the undertones as well as for the melody.

Thankful may I ever be for benefits both great and small—and never fail in gratitude for that divinest gift of all: the love of friends that I have known in times of failure and success. O may the first prayer of the day be always one of thankfulness.

Patience Strong

God's Been Good To Me

In a sense every season is Thanksgiving season. Following from the harvest theme that ultimately it is God who gives us our abundance from the ground and from our daily experiences, each fall we come to God with special thanks. One such artistic comment on God's blessings comes from a poem by Clay Harrison:

> I'm mindful of the blessings
> that come my way each day.
> My heart is overflowing
> each time I kneel to pray.
>
> I'm thankful for the seasons;
> each one's a masterpiece.
> I'm allowed to work the land,
> but God still holds the lease.
>
> I'm grateful for the friendships
> that brighten sorrow's way.
> Because my cup of happiness
> sustains me every day.
>
> I'm grateful for eyes that see
> the beauty of it all.
> Because God's been good to me
> and blessed me through it all.
>
> I'm thankful for the little things
> that fill my life with love.
> The best things in life are free;
> they come from God above!

Clay Harrison

Irish Prayer

My Irish relatives help me understand this prayer of St. Patrick. For me Patrick is covering all his bets, trying to tie securely the tarpaulin on the ship of life sailing with no small risk through the narrows of rock-strewn channels.

> Christ, be with me, Christ before me, Christ behind me,
> Christ in me, Christ beneath me, Christ above me,
> Christ on my right, Christ on my left,
> Christ where I lie, Christ where I sit, Christ where I arise,
> Christ in the heart of every one who thinks of me,
> Christ in the mouth of every one who speaks of me,
> Christ in every eye that sees me,
> Christ in every ear that hears me.
>> Salvation is of the Lord,
>> Salvation is of the Lord,
>> Salvation is of the Christ,
>> May your salvation, O Lord, be ever with us.

St. Patrick

Prayer from Kenya

One poet said that courage is fear that has said its prayers. Facing up to life is not always easy. Prayer is our means to look to God for assistance. Below is a prayer from Kenya addressing the need to always seek out truth in our lives.

From the cowardice that dare not face new truth,
From the laziness that is contented with half truth,
From the arrogance that thinks it knows all truth,
Good Lord, deliver me.

The Oxford Book of Prayers

Prayer from India

No one wants to admit despair. Why? It is the opposite of hope, and all believers are expected to hope. Yet, indeed sometimes we sink into the very depths of despair wondering where our God is. This prayer from India gives us consolation for all those dark days and nights of life's experiences.

Like an ant on a stick both ends of which are burning, I go to and fro without knowing what to do and in great despair. Like the inescapable shadow which follows me, the dead weight of sin haunts me. Graciously look upon me. Thy love is my refuge.

The Oxford Book of Prayers

Needs and Wants

We move through life with hopes and dreams that often take the form of wants and desires. Soon we learn to distinguish what we need for a normal human life from what we want for a life that yields to superfluous desires. The struggle is constant: "What do I need; what do I want? Are the two the same?" There is the Chinese proverb that runs thus:

Have mercy on me, O beneficent One, I was angered for I had no shoes: Then I met a man who had no feet.

The Oxford Book of Prayers

4. December Prayers

Our Advent Life on Earth
The Messiah Comes as an Infant

Teach Us the Way

The Chinook Indians lived on Puget Sound long before Boeing built its 747 and long before the timber barons cut away the trees from the edge of Elliot Bay. If the Chinook prayed for an understanding of how we are to follow the "way" of the Great Spirit, we today deserve to repeat the same humble prayer.

We call upon the earth, our planet home, with its beautiful depths and soaring heights, its vitality and abundance of life, and together we ask that it:

Teach us, and show us the way.

We call upon the mountains, the Cascades and the Olympics, the high green valleys and meadows filled with wild flowers, the snows that never melt, the summits of intense silence, and we ask that they:

Teach us, and show us the way.

We call upon the waters that rim the earth, horizon to horizon, that flow in our rivers and streams, that fall upon our gardens and fields, and we ask that they:

Teach us, and show us the way.

We call upon the land which grows our food, the nurturing soil, and fertile fields, the abundant gardens and orchards, and we ask that they:

Teach us, and show us the way.

PRAYER ONE

We call upon the forests, the great trees reaching
strongly to the sky with earth in their roots and
the heavens in their branches, the fir and the
pine and the cedar, and we ask them to:

Teach us, and show us the way.

We call upon the creatures of the fields and forests
and the seas, our brothers and sisters the
wolves and deer, the eagle and dove, the great
whales and the dolphin, the beautiful Orca and
salmon who share our Northwest home, and
we ask them to:

Teach us, and show us the way.

We call upon all those who have lived on this earth,
our ancestors and our friends, who dreamed
the best for future generations, and upon
whose lives our lives are built, and with
thanksgiving, we call upon them to:

Teach us, and show us the way.

And lastly, we call upon all that we hold most
sacred, the presence and power of the Great
Spirit of love and truth which flows through
all the universe . . . to be with us to:

Teach us, and show us the way.

Chinook Blessing Litany
Earth Prayers

PRAYER TWO

Vision of Peace

Like other such passages in the prophets of old, here in Isaiah is a constant call for peace in our world.

In days to come
the mountain of the Lord's house
shall be established as the highest of the
mountains,
and shall be raised above the hills;
all the nations shall stream to it.
Many peoples shall come and say,
"Come, let us go up to the mountain of the Lord,
to the house of the God of Jacob;
that he may teach us his ways
and that we may walk in his paths."
For out of Zion shall go forth instruction,
and the word of the Lord from
Jerusalem.
He shall judge between the nations,
and shall arbitrate for many peoples;
they shall beat their swords into
plowshares,
and their spears into pruning hooks;
nation shall not lift up sword against nation,
neither shall they learn war any more.

Isaiah 2:2-4

Human Growth

Slowly, by long evolutionary development, the human person learned to reflect that she not only could survive, but more significantly could reason. That joyful realization touched the imagination of Carl Sandberg.

> **Once having marched**
> **Over the margins of animal necessity,**
> **Over the grim line of sheer subsistence**
> **Then mankind came**
> **To the deeper rituals of his bones,**
> **To the lights lighter than any bones,**
> **To the time for thinking things over,**
> **To the dance, the song, the story,**
> **Or the hours given over to dreaming,**
> **Once having so marched.**

From "The People Will Live On"
Carl Sandberg (1878–1967)

PRAYER FOUR

Use of Riches

Sometimes we need a message that is clear and straightforward from Scripture. Paul gives us one such message in his First Letter to Timothy.

As for those who in the present age are rich, command them not to be haughty, or to set their hopes on the uncertainty of riches, but rather on God who richly provides us with everything for our enjoyment. They are to do good, to be rich in good works, generous, and ready to share, thus storing up for themselves the treasure of a good foundation for the future, so that they may take hold of the life that really is life.

1 Timothy 6:17-19

Prayer for Help

In the classroom or without, here is a prayer we all pray ever so often in the deepest recesses of our heart:

> **Give me, O Lord, the strength to see my weakness**
> **For what it truly is—and to recognize the need**
> **To lean upon you through others, and to support**
> **them in turn.**
>
> **Stretch me, Lord, that I may learn my limits and**
> **Grow beyond who I am at this moment, drawing**
> **Always nearer to you through those around me.**

Charles Rousseau

A Candle

The craft of making candles is lost to most of us. Museum and Renaissance fairs remind us of this ancient practice, but we forget that even today, we, on occasion, have need of candles for light. The unknown author below compares the making of a candle with our individual spiritual life.

A candle's but a simple thing
It starts with just a bit of string.
But dipped and dipped with
      patient hand
It gathers wax upon the strand
Until complete and snowy white
It gives at last a lovely light.
Life seems so like that bit of string
Each deed we do a simple thing
Yet day by day if on life's strand
We work with patient heart
      and hand
It gathers joy, makes Dark days
      bright
And gives at last a lovely light.

Anonymous

Concern for Neighbor

We deserve to reflect on the polar ideas of rich and poor as experiences that we normally will have in our adult life. Without necessarily suffering any great spiritual hardship, and without a sense of error or guilt, we ought to see life as providing many plus and minus experiences simply because a variety of events occur in everyone's daily life. Paul, in his warm correspondence with the Philippians, reveals his deep personal gratitude upon receiving their support during his personal experience of shortage and plenty.

I rejoice in the Lord greatly that now at last you have revived your concern for me; indeed, you were concerned for me, but had no opportunity to show it. Not that I am referring to being in need; for I have learned to be content with whatever I have. I know what it is to have little, and I know what it is to have plenty. In any and all circumstances I have learned the secret of being well-fed and of going hungry, of having plenty and of being in need. I can do all things through him who strengthens me. In any case, it was kind of you to share my distress.

Philippians 4:10-14

The Proper Time

Both the English and the Italians have one rich word in common "proper" or "proprio." This word evokes a warm response from the human emotions in our hearts. We admit, then deny, that this is the proper time. What is difficult or seemingly negative, we avoid; yet it may be the proper time, such as death. What is easy and joyful we readily embrace, knowing that this joy, although proper and appropriate, is passing and limited regardless how meaningful and significant to our total life at the moment. Slowly we repeat these words of the preacher Qoheleth.

> **For everything there is a season, and a time**
> **for every matter under heaven:**
> **a time to be born, and a time to die;**
> **a time to plant, and a time to pluck up what is**
> **planted;**
> **a time to kill, and a time to heal;**
> **a time to break down, and a time to build up;**
> **a time to weep, and a time to laugh;**
> **a time to mourn, and a time to dance;**
> **a time to throw away stones, and a time to gather**
> **stones together;**
> **a time to embrace, and a time to refrain from**
> **embracing;**
>
> **a time to seek, and a time to lose;**
> **a time to keep, and a time to throw away;**
> **a time to tear, and a time to sew;**
> **a time to keep silence, and a time to speak;**
> **a time to love, and a time to hate;**
> **a time for war, and a time for peace.**

Ecclesiastes 3:1-8

Dignity of Human Life

The writer of Psalm 8 reflects that when he looks up at the heavens, the moon and the stars, he not only sees a reason for reflecting on the majesty of God as the Creator, but he also can compare these heavenly wonders with the wonder of human life.

When you and I forget our awesome dignity as creatures of God, a little less than the gods, i.e. considered to be members of the heavenly court of YHWH, we forget what life is all about. Our harmony with the universe, our unity with God who created us, are reflections that must frequently enter our daily lives. Else, our time spent on earth becomes more puzzling than it deserves to be.

O LORD, our Sovereign,
   how majestic is your name in all the earth!

You have set your glory above the heavens.
   Out of the mouths of babes and infants
you have founded a bulwark because of your foes,
   to silence the enemy and the avenger.
When I look at your heavens, the work of
     your fingers,
   the moon and the stars that you have
     established;
what are human beings that you are
     mindful of them,
   mortals that you care for them?

Yet you have made them a little lower than God,
   and crowned them with glory and honor.
You have given them dominion over the
     works of your hands;

you have put all things under their feet,
all sheep and oxen,
and also the beasts of the field,
the birds of the air, and the fish of the sea,
whatever passes along the paths of the seas.

O LORD, our Sovereign,
how majestic is your name in all the earth!

Psalm 8

Threshold Prayer

Scientists of religion tell us that crossing the threshold is a sacred experience. By this act we enter the sacred space of a family—significant enough to visit. Below is a prayer that reflects on this common yet strangely important experience.

> **O God,**
> **make the door of this house wide enough**
> **to receive all who need human love and**
> **fellowship, and a heavenly Father's care;**
> **and narrow enough to shut out**
> **all envy, pride and hate.**
> **Make its threshold smooth enough**
> **to be no stumbling-block to children,**
> **nor to straying feet,**
> **but rugged enough to turn back**
> **the tempter's power:**
> **make it a gateway**
> **to thine eternal kingdom.**

> *Bishop Thomas Ken (1637–1711)*

The World Is Too Much with Us

Sometimes we simply wish to escape the world. Even without the academic training of a space-scientist, we are tempted to abandon the planet earth and start fresh on another planet such as Mars. One small detail holds us back. Such a migration would be very expensive. As earth-bound and oxygen-breathing, we cannot readily leave. So, we make peace with our surroundings and try to live as humanly as possible for children of God meant ultimately for heaven, the ultimate in space travel.

William Wordsworth cautions us not to embrace the world without reflection, and restraint, not merely exist as buyers and sellers of goods. With a solid Christian approach we listen to Wordsworth and take inventory of our own personal life.

> **The world is too much with us; late and soon,**
> **Getting and spending, we lay waste our powers:**
> **Little we see in Nature that is ours;**
> **We have given our hearts away, a sordid boon!**

> *William Wordsworth*

My Gift

Gift giving is a basic custom at Christmas. The obvious danger of going overboard with that aspect of the season looms always in the background. We know that the material aspects of gift giving could do damage to the warm spirit of the custom. We continue to ask: If Christ is the ultimate gift of Christmas, where does our gift giving belong? A poem by Christina Rossetti puts us safely on track during the Christmas season.

> **What can I give Him**
> **Poor as I am?**
> **If I were a shepherd,**
> **I would give Him a lamb,**
> **If I were a Wise Man,**
> **I would do my part—**
> **But what can I give Him,**
> **Give my heart.**

Christina G. Rossetti (1830–1894)

PRAYER THREE

Childlike Care

Christ exalts the role of the child in the Christian life, and urges us to become spiritually as children in order to enter (usually in old age) the kingdom of heaven. A French prayer that inspires us to childlike sensitivity.

> **Grant me, O God,**
> **the heart of a child,**
> **pure and transparent as a spring;**
> **a simple heart,**
> **which never harbors sorrows;**
> **a heart glorious in self-giving,**
> **tender in compassion;**
> **a heart faithful and generous,**
> **which will never forget any good**
> **or bear a grudge for any evil.**
> **Make me a heart gentle and humble,**
> **loving without asking any return,**
> **large-hearted and undauntable,**
> **which no ingratitude can sour**
> **and no indifference can weary;**
> **a heart penetrated by the love of Jesus**
> **whose desire will only be satisfied in heaven.**
>
> **Grant me, O Lord,**
> **the mind and heart**
> **of thy dear Son.**

The Oxford Book of Prayers

Christmas Prayers

Robert Louis Stevenson reflects on the meaning of Christmas that flows from the Gospel story. He says:

O God, our loving Father, help us rightly to remember the birth of Jesus, that we may share in the song of the angels, the gladness of the shepherds, the worship of the wise men. Close the door to hate, and open the door of love all over the world. Let kindness come with every gift and good desires with every greeting. Deliver us from evil by the blessing that Christ brings, and teach us to be merry with clean hearts. May the Christmas morning make us happy to be thy children and the Christmas evening bring us to our beds with grateful thoughts, forgiving and forgiven, for Jesus' sake. Amen.

Robert Louis Stevenson

Mother of God

Our understanding of God is necessarily incomplete. However, our appreciation of God grows by degrees with an accompanying sense of connectedness. God is related to us in the best of images that we can produce, such as: friend, father, mother, care giver, counselor, etc. We reflect on Mary, the mother of Jesus in this following prayer to help us appreciate the infinite love of our God, the creator of gender, both masculine and feminine.

> **Woman was born of You, Mother God,**
> **yet Jesus was born of a woman**
> **whom we call,**
> **mother of God.**
> **Mother God of the mother of God,**
> **we praise You**
> **as we struggle to comprehend**
> **Your incomprehensible ways.**
> **May we who are sister of Mary**
> **take part in her God-bearing,**
> **God-sharing spirit**
> **for Your greater glory and praise,**
> **now and forever.**
>
> **Amen.**

Miriam Therese Winter

One Solitary Life

As we approach Christmas or Easter, I am reminded of an essay about Jesus Christ. Like so much literature the author is anonymous.

Here is a young man who was born in an obscure village, the child of a peasant woman. He grew up in another village. He worked in a carpenter shop until he was thirty, and then for three years he was an itinerant preacher. He never wrote a book. He never held an office. He never owned a home. He never had a family. He never went to a college. He never put his foot inside a big city. He never travelled two hundred miles from the place he was born. He never did one of the things that usually accompany greatness. He had no credentials but himself.

While he was still a young man, the tide of public opinion turned against him. His friends ran away. He was handed over to his enemies. He went through the mockery of a trial. He was nailed to a cross, between two thieves. While he was dying, his executioners gambled for the only piece of property he had on earth, and that was his coat. When he was dead, he was laid in a borrowed grave through the pity of a friend. Nineteen centuries wide have come and gone, and today he is the central figure of the human race, and the leader of the column of progress.

I am far within the mark when I say that all the armies that ever marched, and all the navies that

PRAYER ONE

ever sailed, and all the parliaments that ever sat,
and all the kings that ever reigned, put together,
have not affected the life of man upon this earth as
has that One Solitary Life.

Anonymous

A Christmas Meditation

A powerful meditation about the miracle of Christmas deserves to be heard within these last days before Christmas. The author is an English teacher from Seattle.

We gather to celebrate the advent of Christmas.
We look forward to an event that's already taken
     place.
We look back and contemplate what is still to come.
A mystery outside of time enfolds us.

Emmanuel,
God With Us,
Is with us
As we are now.

We're aware of our redemption, but we're also only
     too aware
Of our weakness and our sin.
Christ is gentle with us at Christmas,
Presenting himself to us as a human child, a
     newborn
Whom we haven't yet had a chance
To hurt.
Before Easter, we must face the truth of human
     cruelty, ignorance, blindness.
We must walk through the crucifixion and recognize
That our voices mingle with the taunts of the
     maddened crowd,
That our hands hold scourges
And place the crown of thorns.

But before the newborn baby Jesus in the stable at
     Bethlehem,
We need face
Only our hope.

We step quietly with the good shepherds, and our
     best instincts
Are called forth.
We can see ourselves reaching out to cradle the
     child
In our arms, to speak the tender nonsense words
That will coax into radiance
The divine infant's smile.

Like babies ourselves, we stretch out our hands
Towards all that glitters and is bright.
We return to the dream of innocence.
The veil of heaven opens.
We are bathed in the starlight of love.
Night's shadows flee from our safe circle,
And through our veins rushes the thrill
Of vivid, present joy.
We are one with God who is one with us.
We're all strong and good and giving to each other
And to the baby who is God
Who lets us hold him.

Margaret Holland

Sharon's Christmas Prayer

To see Christmas through the eyes of a young child gives us a
special understanding of the feast. This understanding comes as
an unexpected gift at Christmas.

> She was five, sure of the facts,
> and recited them with slow solemnity,
> convinced every word was revelation.
> She said
> they were so poor they had only
> peanut butter and jelly sandwiches to eat
> and they went a long way from home
> without getting lost. The lady rode
> a donkey, the man walked, and the baby
> was inside the lady.
> They had to stay in a stable
> with an ox and an ass (hee-hee)
> but the Three Rich Men found them
> because a star lighted the roof.
> Shepherds came and you could
> pet the sheep but not feed them.
> Then the baby was borned.
> And do you know who he was?
> Her quarter eyes inflated
> to silver dollars.
> The baby was God.
> And she jumped in the air,
> whirled round, dove into a sofa,
> and buried her head under the cushion
> which is the only proper response
> to the Good News of the Incarnation.

John Shea

Christmas

God's glory, now, is kindled gentler than low
   candlelight
Under the rafters of a barn.
Eternal Peace is sleeping in the hay,
And wisdom's born in secret in a straw-roofed
   stable.
And O! Make holy music in the stars, you happy
   angels;
You shepherds, gather on the hill.

From Collected Poems
Thomas Merton

Christmas

The compelling message of Christmas carries over into the new year. The following prayer repeats the Christmas challenge to each of us as we celebrate this feast of light and life.

> "When the song of
> the angels is stilled;
> When the star
> in the sky is gone;
> When the kings
> and priests are home;
> When the shepherds
> are back with their flocks. . . .
>
> The work of
> Christmas begins. . . .
> To find the lost,
> To heal the broken,
> To feed the hungry,
> To release the prisoner,
> To rebuild the nations,
> To bring peace among peoples. . . .
> To make music in the heart!"

5. *January Prayers*

New Year
New Start
Hope Within
New Resolutions

A Guide to a Happy Life

Quotable quotes, maxims, aphorisms, and clever "one liners" abound at the end of every old year to help prepare us for the new year. A few years ago the following "Guide to a Happy Life" appeared in the *Sunday Oregonian*. We can readily accept one or more of these maxims as appropriate for our own new year's resolutions.

No one will ever get out of this world alive. Resolve therefore to maintain a reasonable sense of values.

Take care of yourself. Good health is one major source of wealth. Without it, happiness is more difficult to achieve.

Resolve to be cheerful and helpful. People will repay you in kind.

Avoid angry, abrasive persons. They are generally vengeful.

Avoid zealots. They are generally humorless.

Resolve to listen more and talk less. No one ever learns anything by talking.

Be chary of giving advice. Wise men don't need it and fools won't heed it.

Resolve to be tender with the young, compassionate with the aged, sympathetic with the striving and tolerant of the weak and wrong. Sometime in life you will have been all of these.

Do not equate money with success. There are many successful moneymakers who are miserable failures as human beings. What counts most about success is how a person achieves it.

Attitude

The brief paragraph "attitude" shows us the psychological priority of ATTITUDE among other indicators of virtue and character. Charles Swindoll says:

> "The longer I live, the more I realize the impact of attitude on life. Attitude, to me, is more important than facts. It is more important than the past, than education, than money, than circumstances, than failures, than successes, than what other people think or say or do. It is more important than appearance, giftedness or skill. It will make or break a company . . . a church . . . a home. The remarkable thing is we have a choice every day regarding the attitude we will embrace for that day. We cannot change our past . . . we cannot change the fact that people will act in a certain way. We cannot change the inevitable. The only thing we can do, is play on the one string we have, and that is our attitude . . . I am convinced that life is 10 percent what happens to me and 90 percent how I react to it. And so it is with you . . . we are in charge of our ATTITUDES."

Good News

The word "gospel" means "good news." When Jesus announced for the first time that he was the Messiah, or the Christ, who was destined by his father to bring the *Good News* to all people, the Jewish people were dumfounded. At last the Messiah had come, but is he authentic? Luke describes the event as follows:

When he came to Nazareth, where he had been brought up, he went to the synagogue on the sabbath day, as was his custom. He stood up to read, and the scroll of the prophet Isaiah was given to him. He unrolled the scroll and found the place where it was written:

"The Spirit of the Lord is upon me,
because he has anointed me
to bring good news to the poor.
He has sent me to proclaim release to the captives
and recovery of sight to the blind,
to let the oppressed go free,
to proclaim the year of the Lord's favor."

And he rolled up the scroll, gave it back to the attendant, and sat down. The eyes of all in the synagogue were fixed on him. Then he began to say to them, "Today this scripture has been fulfilled in your hearing." All spoke well of him and were amazed at the gracious words that came from his mouth.

Luke 4:16-22

The Devil and His Friend

Like the search for truth, the search for religious truth is an unending journey. This search moves us to the humble conviction that we are never more than pilgrims on a long journey to heaven, the place of full truth. Anthony de Mello says:

> **The devil once went for a walk with a friend. They saw a man ahead of them stoop down and pick up something from the road.**
>
> **"What did that man find?" asked the friend.**
>
> **"A piece of Truth," said the devil.**
>
> **"Doesn't that disturb you?" asked the friend.**
>
> **"No it does not," said the devil, "I shall allow him to make a religious belief out of it."**

A religious belief is a signpost pointing the way to Truth. People who cling tenaciously to the signpost are prevented from moving towards the Truth because they have the false feeling that they already possess it.

The Song of the Bird

Failure

Many exciting events occurred in the United States in the 1800s, but we do not usually turn to a person in this part of United States history who statistically was considered a failure. Today we will be talking about failure and this person.

Prayerfully we might consider how failure often is a greater blessing than success, and how the difference between a great person and an ordinary person lies in the ability to overcome failures by transferring them to success.

Allow me to read the statistics of this person in the 1800s who failed so dramatically.

Failed in business,	'31
Defeated for legislature,	'32
Failed in business again,	'33
Elected to legislature,	'34
Sweetheart died,	'35
Suffered nervous breakdown,	'36
Defeated for speaker,	'38
Defeated for elector,	'40
Defeated for Congress,	'43
Elected to Congress,	'48
Defeated for Senate,	'55
Defeated for Vice President,	'56
Defeated for Senate,	'58
Elected President of the United States,	'60

The person who made this record of misfortune, crowned by final success, was Abraham Lincoln.

Thomas P. Ramire

I Never Saw a Moor

Emily Dickinson reminds us that we do not need to see a thing to believe it exists. We believe or trust people to tell us the truth. Trust in people is based on believing their testimony that they have seen the object we have never been privileged to see. A Nebraska farmer has not seen the ocean but he trusts that it exists. He trusts the map maker and he trusts his friends who have seen the ocean. With Emily Dickinson we can review all the important things we believe exist, though we have never seen them.

> I never saw a moor,
> I never saw the sea;
> Yet I know how the heather looks,
> And what a wave must be.
>
> I never spoke with God,
> Nor visited in Heaven;
> Yet certain am I of the spot
> As if the chart were given.

Emily Dickinson (1830–1886)

Duty to the Weak

Literature is replete with stories of human beings stepping over other human beings in order to get ahead. Paul, in his Letter to the Romans, reminds us that true Christian motives urge us to go out to our neighbor in friendship and love. In particular, we should be sensitive to our neighbors who are weak or have special needs. He says:

> **We who are strong ought to put up with the failings of the weak, and not to please ourselves. Each of us must please our neighbor for the good purpose of building up the neighbor. For Christ did not please himself; but, as it is written, "The insults of those who insult you have fallen on me." For whatever was written in former days was written for our instruction, so that by steadfastness and by the encouragement of the scriptures we might have hope. May the God of steadfastness and encouragement grant you to live in harmony with one another, in accordance with Christ Jesus, so that together you may with one voice glorify the God and Father of our Lord Jesus Christ.**

Romans 15:1-6

Pure Religion

Regardless of our culture or family background, religion is a most personal issue. For the Jews who so easily could become embroiled in cultural problems, the words of James strike home. Religion is never meant to be a complicated, doctrine-driven experience. In his epistle we read:

Religion that is pure and undefiled before God, the Father, is this: to care for orphans and widows in their distress, and to keep oneself unstained by the world.

James 1:27

A modern-day Eastern description of religion arises from the Dalai Lama who says:

**"My religion is very simple.
My religion is kindness."**

Random Acts of Kindness

PRAYER FOUR

Humility

Pride is a constant subtle force that silently rusts away our spiritual strength. Chesterton offers the following prayer as a check to this subtle force.

> O God of earth and altar,
>   Bow down and hear our cry;
> Our earthly rulers falter,
>   Our people drift and die;
> The walls of gold entomb us,
>   The swords of scorn divide,
> Take not thy thunder from us,
>   But take away our pride.
>
> From all that terror teaches,
>   From lies of tongue and pen,
> From all the easy speeches
>   That comfort cruel men,
> From sale and profanation
>   Of honor and the sword,
> From sleep and from damnation,
>   Deliver us, good Lord!

G.K. Chesterton (1874–1936)

Practical Rules

One Seattle philosopher brings our life into focus with the following comments:

All I really need to know about how to live and what to do and how to be I learned in kindergarten. Wisdom was not at the top of the graduate-school mountain, but there in the sandpile at Sunday School. These are the things I learned:

- **Share everything.**
- **Play fair.**
- **Don't hit people.**
- **Put things back where you found them.**
- **Clean up your own mess.**
- **Don't take things that aren't yours.**
- **Say you're sorry when you hurt somebody.**
- **Wash your hands before you eat.**
- **Flush.**
- **Warm cookies and cold milk are good for you.**
- **Live a balanced life—learn some and think some and draw and paint and sing and dance and play and work every day some.**
- **Take a nap every afternoon.**
- **When you go out into the world, watch out for traffic, hold hands, and stick together.**
- **Be aware of wonder. Remember the little seed in the Styrofoam cup: The roots go down and the**

plant goes up and nobody really knows how or why, but we are all like that.

- Goldfish and hamsters and white mice and even the little seed in the Styrofoam cup—they all die. So do we.

- And then remember the Dick-and-Jane books and the first word you learned—the biggest word of all—LOOK.

Everything you need to know is in there somewhere. The Golden Rule and love and basic sanitation. Ecology and politics and equality and sane living.

Take any one of those items and extrapolate it into sophisticated adult terms and apply it to your family life or your work or your government or your world and it holds true and clear and firm. Think what a better world it would be if we all— the whole world—had cookies and milk about three o-clock every afternoon and then lay down with our blankies for a nap. Or if all governments had as a basic policy to always put things back where they found them and to clean up their own mess.

And it is still true, no matter how old you are— when you go out into the world, it is best to hold hands and stick together.

Robert Fulghum

PRAYER ONE

Joy Known Through Sorrow

The poet Shelley so artistically reminds us how sorrow provides understanding for the rest of our life, especially the joyful occasions. Our teacher in this lesson of life is Jesus, the Incarnate Son of God.

> We look before and after,
>   And pine for what is not:
> Our sincerest laughter
>   With some pain is fraught;
> Our sweetest songs are those that tell of saddest thought.
>
> Yet if we could scorn
>   Hate, and pride, and fear;
> If we were things born
>   Not to shed a tear,
> I know not how thy joy we ever should come near.
>
> Better than all measures
>   Of delightful sound,
> Better than all treasures
>   That in books are found,
> Thy skill to poet were, thou scorner of the ground!
>
> Teach me half the gladness
>   That thy brain must know,
> Such harmonious madness
>   From my lips would flow
> The world should listen then, as I am listening now!

Percy Bysshe Shelley (1792–1822)

PRAYER TWO

Oracle for Peace

The ancient Jews as well as any oppressed people today realized the harshness and irrationality of war. Constantly the prophets like Micah called attention to the avenues for peace—the route people would love to take in order to realize this needed condition for society. Micah says:

In days to come
 the mountain of the Lord's house
shall be established as the highest of the
 mountains,
 and shall be raised up above the hills.
Peoples shall stream to it,
 and many nations shall come and say:
"Come, let us go up to the mountain of the Lord,
 to the house of the God of Jacob;
that he may teach us his ways
 and that we may walk in his paths."

For out of Zion shall go forth instruction,
 and the word of the Lord from
 Jerusalem.
He shall judge between many peoples,
 and shall arbitrate between strong
 nations far away;
they shall beat their swords into
 plowshares,
 and their spears into pruning hooks;
nation shall not lift up sword against nation,
 neither shall they learn war any more;
but they shall all sit under their own vines
 and under their own fig trees,

and no one shall make them afraid;
for the mouth of the Lord of hosts has
spoken.

Micah 4:1-4

Jesus' Prayer for Unity

At the Last Supper Jesus shared his hope-filled prayers with his twelve apostles. The Gospel of John records one passage so revealing for our times. Let us imagine as we slowly read this passage that our Lord's eyes are focused directly on us. One question we must ask ourselves is: "How much do I belong to the world?"

But now I am coming to you, and I speak these things in the world so that they may have my joy made complete in themselves. I have given them your word, and the world has hated them because they do not belong to the world, just as I do not belong to the world. I am not asking you to take them out of the world, but I ask you to protect them from the evil one. They do not belong to the world, just as I do not belong to the world. Sanctify them in the truth; your word is truth. As you have sent me into the world, so I have sent them into the world. And for their sakes I sanctify myself, so that they also may be sanctified in truth.

I ask not only on behalf of these, but also on behalf of those who will believe in me through their word, that they may all be one. As you, Father, are in me and I am in you, may they also be in us, so that the world may believe that you have sent me.

John 17:13-21

Quiet Work

We all want to contribute something lasting to the world. Our desire for immortality is ineluctably linked to do something that will live on after we die. All-in-all, there is pride and selfishness in this desire, but if it comes as an awareness that we are instruments of God meant to accomplish only what God wills, we fit more humbly in the "scheme of things."

One lesson, Nature, let me learn of thee,
One lesson which in every wind is blown,
One lesson of two duties kept at one
Though the loud world proclaim their enmity—
Of toil unsevered from tranquility,
Of labor, that in lasting fruit outgrows
Far noisier schemes, accomplished in repose,
Too great for haste, too high for rivalry!

Yes, while on earth a thousand discords ring,
Man's fitful uproar mingling with his toil,
Still do thy sleepless ministers move on,
Their glorious tasks in silence perfecting;
Still working, blaming still our vain turmoil,
Laborers that shall not fail, when man is gone.

Matthew Arnold (1822–1888)

Oh Yet We Trust

Two young women were talking—an optimist and a pessimist. The optimist said: "This is the best possible world!" The pessimist replied: "I am afraid that you are correct!"

You and I fit into one or the other position, but with a sense of God in our lives, the world makes more sense. Below are some thoughts by Alfred Tennyson about our world.

>Oh yet we trust that somehow good
>>Will be the final goal of ill,
>>To pangs of nature, sins of will,
>Defects of doubt, and taints of blood;
>
>That nothing walks with aimless feet;
>>That not one life shall be destroyed,
>>Or cast as rubbish to the void,
>When God hath made the pile complete;
>
>That not a worm is cloven in vain;
>>That not a moth with vain desire
>>Is shriveled in a fruitless fire,
>Or but subserves another's gain.
>
>Behold, we know not anything;
>>We can but trust that good shall fall
>>At last—far off—at last, to all
>And every winter change to spring.
>
>So runs my dream; but what am I?
>>An infant crying in the night:
>>An infant crying for the light:
>And with no language but a cry.

Alfred Tennyson (1809–1892)

121

Let It Be Forgotten

The discipline of learning how to forget things, events, circumstances is a harsh discipline. Poets and philosophers alike suggest that our life is richer if we learn to forget certain events from the past.

Let it be forgotten, as a flower is forgotten,
   Forgotten as a fire that once was singing gold,
Let it be forgotten for ever and ever,
   Time is a kind friend, he will make us old.

If anyone asks, say it was forgotten
   Long and long ago,
As a flower, as a fire, as a hushed footfall
   In a long-forgotten snow.

Sara Teasdale (1884–1933)

PRAYER TWO

God's Gift

Julian of Norwich stands in the great company of mystics and theologians who assist us in understanding the place of prayer in our lives. She tells us of the rewards of going to God in simplicity and sincerity without rehearsing a special list of petitions. In her private revelations she learned that knowing the goodness of God is the highest knowledge. The core prayer she prays is the bold prayer:

God of your goodness, give me yourself, for you are sufficient for me. I cannot properly ask for anything less to be worthy of you. If I should ask less I would always be in want. In you alone do I have all.

Chapter 5, Revelations of Divine Love

A similar prayer comes to mind from the region of Northern Bengal:

If I ask him for a gift, he will give it to me, and then I shall have to go away. But I don't want to go away. Give me no gift—give me thyself. I want to be with thee, my beloved.

*Ascribed to the oral tradition of
a hill tribe in Northern Bengal*

The Hound of Heaven

Another approach to the prayer of Julian of Norwich and of the Northern Bengal Christians is found in Francis Thompson's poem "The Hound of Heaven."

I fled Him, down the nights and down the days;
    I fled Him, down the arches of the years;
I fled Him, down the labyrinthine ways
    Of my own mind; and in the mist of tears
I hid from Him, and under running laughter.
        Up vistaed hopes I sped;
        And shot, precipitated,
Adown Titanic glooms of chasmed fears,
    From those strong Feet that followed, followed
        after
            But with unhurrying chase,
            And unperturbed pace,
    Deliberate speed, majestic instancy,
        They beat—and a Voice beat
        More instant than the Feet—
"All things betray thee, who betrayed Me."

    I pleaded, outlaw-wise,
By many a hearted casement, curtained red,
    Trellised with intertwining charities
For, though I knew His love Who followed,
    Yet was I sore adread
Lest, having Him, I must have naught beside.

From "The Hound of Heaven"
Francis Thompson (1859–1907)

PRAYER FOUR

Childlike Love

Jesus told us to allow the children to come to him for "such was the kingdom of heaven." A story of a young boy gives meaning to Jesus' thought. One day a four-year-old boy picked some dandelions and brought them to his mother. The kind-hearted mother naturally accepted these with joy, but she did more—she put them in a small vase and centered the vase on the dining room table for all the family to see at the evening meal. An alert observer will find many lessons here of mother love and of a child's devotion. Moreover, the story points out the depth of Teresa of Avila's statement:

God doesn't want our deeds;
God wants the love that prompts them.

PRAYER FIVE

Snow

After a worrisome lament God reminds Job that the Creator is in charge of the universe and that Job need not worry. God tells Job among other things how snow is a gift serving a special purpose.

Have you entered the storehouses of the snow,
or have you seen the storehouses of the hail,
which I have reserved for the time of trouble,
for the day of battle and war?

Job 38:22-23

6. February Prayers

"The Longest Month of the Year"??

Pride—Service

One day the apostles showed Jesus how pride was getting in the way of their dedication to God's will. Jesus met the issue in his traditional calm manner.

A dispute arose among them as to which one of them was to be regarded as the greatest. But he said to them, "The kings of the Gentiles lord it over them; and those in authority over them are called benefactors. But not so with you; rather the greatest among you must become like the youngest, and the leader like one who serves. For who is greater, the one who is at the table or the one who serves? Is it not the one at the table? But I am among you as one who serves.

Luke 22:24-27

PRAYER TWO

True Spirituality

Cardinal Newman said: "To live is to change." Many good people resist change in the name of a need to develop the good qualities they possess. However, if living is a process, and change is a basic element in our life, we somehow must learn how to put change into our own spirituality. Anthony de Mello gives us a brief meditation.

The Master was asked, "What is Spirituality?"

He said, "Spirituality is that which succeeds in bringing man to Inner Transformation."

"But if I apply the traditional methods handed down by the Masters, is that not Spirituality?"

"It is not Spirituality if it does not perform its function for you. A blanket is no longer a blanket if it does not keep you warm."

"So Spirituality does change?"

"People change and needs change. So what was Spirituality once is Spirituality no more. What generally goes under the name of Spirituality is merely the record of past methods."

Cut the coat to fit the person. Don't cut the person to fit the coat.

The Song of the Bird

The Good Shepherd

I suppose if you asked the ordinary person on the street to recite one psalm that he knew, he would announce that it was Psalm 23. The institutional Church uses this psalm to console the bereaved and the downtrodden, but you and I find personal support in it for all types of experiences of daily living.

> The LORD is my shepherd, I shall not want.
>   He makes me lie down in green pastures;
> he leads me beside still waters;
>   he restores my soul.
> He leads me in right paths
>   for his name's sake.
>
> Even though I walk through the darkest valley,
>   I fear no evil;
> for you are with me;
>   your rod and your staff—
>   they comfort me.
>
> You prepare a table before me
>   in the presence of my enemies;
> you anoint my head with oil;
>   my cup overflows.
> Surely goodness and mercy shall follow me
>   all the days of my life,
> and I shall dwell in the house of the LORD
>   my whole life long.

Psalm 23

PRAYER FOUR

Work Prayer for a Busy Person

As a paraphrase to Psalm 23, the following prayer for a busy person is especially suited to our American societal value system. Now, more than in the past, we are people bent on speed, efficiency, and accomplishment. The slayer lurking in the background is our growing materialistic view of life. We hurry to make money while neglecting to contemplate the riches of nature appreciated only at a pace that is slower than that to which most of us Americans have grown accustomed.

**The Lord is my pace-setter. I shall not rush.
He makes me stop and rest for quiet intervals. He
provides me with images of stillness which restore
my serenity. He leads me in ways of efficiency
through calmness of mind.**

**His guidance is peace even though I have a great
many things to accomplish. I will not fret, for his
presence is here. He prepares refreshment and
renewal in the midst of my activities by anointing
me with His oils of tranquility.**

**My cup of joyous energy overflows. Surely, harmony
and effectiveness shall be the fruit of my hours. I
shall walk in the pace of the Lord and dwell in his
house forever.**

Anonymous

Trust in Eternity

The average person does not want to die. Depending on our attitude, each of us approaches death with a certain level of fear or apprehension, or lack of trust. Ideally, if we are Jews or Christians, we look forward to death because death means that we enter a new life, one filled with the presence of God and all that God offers his beloved creatures.

William Cullen Bryant recommended the following as an abiding attitude toward death:

> **So live, that when thy summons comes to join**
> **The innumerable caravan, which moves**
> **To that mysterious realm, where each shall take**
> **His chamber in the silent halls of death.**
> **Thou go not, like the quarry-slave at night,**
> **Scourged to his dungeon, but, sustained and soothed**
> **By an unfaltering trust, approach thy grave**
> **Like one who wraps the drapery of his couch**
> **About him, and lies down to pleasant dreams.**

From "Thanotopsis"
William Cullen Bryant (1794–1878)

Prayer for Mercy

In the Office of the Dead, the official prayer of the Church for its deceased, at the hour of prime, Psalm 51, called the *Miserere,* is recited. This psalm is so consoling and rich in thought that the Christian community does not restrict its use to the prayers for the dead. We use this psalm on all sorts of occasions that touch us with the mystery of life.

There are ten stanzas or nineteen verses in this psalm, yet any solitary verse gives ample food for thought. In time, one or another stanza or verse becomes remembered as especially suited to our growing spiritual lives.

> **Have mercy on me, O God,**
> **according to your steadfast love;**
> **according to your abundant mercy**
> **blot out my transgressions.**
> **Wash me thoroughly from my iniquity,**
> **and cleanse me from my sin.**
>
> **For I know my transgressions,**
> **and my sin is ever before me.**
> **Against you, you alone, have I sinned,**
> **and done what is evil in your sight,**
> **so that you are justified in your sentence**
> **and blameless when you pass judgment.**
> **Indeed, I was born guilty,**
> **a sinner when my mother conceived me.**
>
> **You desire truth in the inward being;**
> **therefore teach me wisdom in my secret heart.**
> **Purge me with hyssop, and I shall be clean;**
> **wash me, and I shall be whiter than snow.**

PRAYER ONE

Let me hear joy and gladness;
   let the bones that you have crushed rejoice.
Hide your face from my sins,
   and blot out all my iniquities.

Create in me a clean heart, O God,
   and put a new and right spirit within me.
Do not cast me away from your presence,
   and do not take your holy spirit from me.
Restore to me the joy of your salvation,
   and sustain in me a willing spirit.
Then I will teach transgressors your ways,
   and sinners will return to you.
Deliver me from bloodshed, O God,
   O God of my salvation,
   and my tongue will sing aloud of your
     deliverance.

O Lord, open my lips,
   and my mouth will declare your praise.
For you have no delight in sacrifice;
   if I were to give a burnt offering, you
     would not be pleased.
The sacrifice acceptable to God is a
     broken spirit;
   a broken and contrite heart, O God, you
     will not despise.

Do good to Zion in your good pleasure;
   rebuild the walls of Jerusalem,
then you will delight in right sacrifices,
   in burnt offerings and whole burnt
     offerings;
then bulls will be offered on your altar.

Psalm 51

Service

So many of us wait around to find our niche in life. Somehow the search is not always successful. We cannot figure out how we can reach our destiny. As we edge towards discouragement, we recall the words of Albert Schweitzer.

"I don't know what your destiny will be, but one thing I do know: the only ones among you who will be really happy are those who have sought and found how to serve."

Mercy

Humility as a sensitivity that we need God if we are going to lead a virtuous life is so basic to Christian living. The parable of the Pharisee and the Publican is a beautiful message at the core of the Gospel message.

> He also told this parable to some who trusted in themselves that they were righteous and regarded others with contempt: "Two men went up to the temple to pray, one a Pharisee and the other a tax collector. The Pharisee, standing by himself, was praying thus, 'God, I thank you that I am not like other people: thieves, rogues, adulterers, or even like this tax collector. I fast twice a week; I give a tenth of all my income.' But the tax collector, standing far off, would not even look up to heaven, but was beating his breast and saying, 'God be merciful to me, a sinner!' I tell you, this man went down to his home justified rather than the other; for all who exalt themselves will be humbled, but all who humble themselves will be exalted."

Luke 18:9-14

Power of God

It is one thing to believe in a God; it is quite another to want God, as the Word made flesh, to show His power in our daily lives. Miriam Winter speaks for all of us in this brief poetic prayer:

> O Word,
> power,
> nurturing space,
> unspeakable
> splendor,
> visible trace
> of love
> loving us
> face
> to face.
> Cult
> of all culture
> in Whom
> we place
> our ultimate
> yearning,
> divine
> discerning
> turning point
> Thou,
> flesh of our
> flesh
> now,
> showing us all
> how
> claim to powers

PRAYER FOUR

**of transforming
heartwarming
grace
is ours.**

Miriam Therese Winter

With You a Part of Me

George Santayana, poet and philosopher, mourned the loss of a close friend. He turned a generally negative experience into a positive impression to store away in his memory. When you and I lose a friend we might turn to this consoling poem.

> With you a part of me hath passed away;
> For in the peopled forest of my mind
> A tree made leafless by this wintry wind
> Shall never don again its green array.
>
> Chapel and fireside, country road and bay,
> Have something of their friendliness resigned;
> Another, If I would, I could not find,
> And I am grown much older in a day.
> But yet I treasure in my memory
> Your gift of charity, and young heart's ease,
> And the dear honor of your amity;
> For these once mine, my life is rich with these.
> And I scarce know which part may greater be—
> What I keep of you, or you rob from me.

George Santayana (1863–1952)

PRAYER ONE

An Invitation from God

Every word from God is an invitation to a type of faith, in God's love, God's care, God's power. Isaiah in chapter 55 speaks eloquently of the ways in which God invites us to life. God invites the poor, the oppressed, the refugees of every conflict. God asks us all simply to listen.

Everyone who thirsts,
    come to the waters;
and you that have no money,
    come, buy and eat!
Come, buy wine and milk
    without money and without price.
Why do you spend your money for that
      which is not bread,
    and your labor for that which does not satisfy?
Listen carefully to me, and eat what is good,
    and delight yourselves in rich food . . .

Seek the LORD while he may be found,
    and call upon him while he is near;
let the wicked forsake their way,
    and the unrighteous their thoughts;
let them return to the LORD, that he may
      have mercy on them,
    and to our God, for he will abundantly pardon.
For my thoughts are not your thoughts,
    nor are your ways my ways, says the Lord.
For as the heavens are higher than the earth,
    so are my ways higher than your ways
    and my thoughts than your thoughts.

PRAYER ONE

For as the rain and the snow come down from
  heaven,
 and do not return there until they have
  watered the earth,
making it bring forth and sprout,
 giving seed to the sower and bread to the eater,
so shall my word be that goes out from my mouth;
 it shall not return to me empty,
but it shall accomplish that which I purpose,
 and succeed in the thing for which I sent it.

Isaiah 55:1, 2, 6-11

Unity in the Spirit

Most of the time we do not consider life as a vocation. Yet, ideally, God, our creator, calls us to live first, then enhance that life by choosing always the highest of values. Paul, the apostle, reflects during his leisure time as a Roman prisoner.

I therefore, the prisoner in the Lord, beg you to lead a life worthy of the calling to which you have been called, with all humility and gentleness, with patience, bearing with one another in love, making every effort to maintain the unity of the Spirit in the bond of peace. There is one body and one Spirit, just as you were called to the one hope of your calling, one Lord, one faith, one baptism, one God and Father of all, who is above all and through all and in all.

Ephesians 4:1-6

143

The Messiah as a Suffering Servant of God

The adventure of Christian faith is filled with the desire to learn about the person of Jesus Christ. Because his role and destiny were so noble we easily might forget that part of his role in life was to suffer. Not a very pleasant news item! Not easily fitted into the Good News! Yet, we as followers of Jesus find such strength in the knowledge that he suffered, and that his suffering had a distinct value tied to our redemption.

See, my servant shall prosper;
   he shall be exalted and lifted up,
   and shall be very high.
Just as there were many who were astonished at him
   —so marred was his appearance,
      beyond human semblance,
   and his form beyond that of mortals—
so shall he startle many nations;
   kings shall shut their mouths because of him;
for that which had not been told them they
      shall see,
   and that which they had not heard they
      shall contemplate.
Who has believed what we have heard?
And to whom has the arm of the LORD
      been revealed?
For he grew up before him like a young plant,
   and like a root out of dry ground;
he had no form or majesty that we should
      look at him,
   nothing in his appearance that we should
      desire him.

PRAYER THREE

He was despised and rejected by others;
    a man of suffering and acquainted with infirmity;
and as one from whom others hide their faces
    he was despised, and we held him of no account.

Surely he has borne our infirmities
    and carried our diseases;
yet we accounted him stricken,
    struck down by God, and afflicted.
But he was wounded for our transgressions,
    crushed for our iniquities;
upon him was the punishment that made us whole,
    and by his bruises we are healed.
All we like sheep have gone astray;
    we have all turned to our own way,
and the Lord has laid on him
    the iniquity of us all.

He was oppressed, and he was afflicted,
    yet he did not open his mouth;
like a lamb that is led to the slaughter,
    and like a sheep that before its shearers is silent,
    so he did not open his mouth.
By a perversion of justice he was taken away.
    Who could have imagined his future?
For he was cut off from the land of the living,
    stricken for the transgression of my people.
They have made his grave with the wicked
    and his tomb with the rich,
although he had done no violence,
    and there was no deceit in his mouth.

Isaiah 52:13-15; 53:1-9

PRAYER FOUR

Timing and Patience

For a comedian timing is everything; so too in life. Many imaginative entrepreneurs move too fast only to be faced with a debt-ridden wait. An old Chinese proverb reads:

Patience is power.
With time and patience
the mulberry leaf becomes silk.

Humility of Christ

Paul relates how the generosity of God is focused on the coming of the Messiah. When Jesus took on human nature, he emptied himself of all his divine characteristics to become like us, and furthermore, to die for us. His entire public life as described in the Gospels unfolds the mystery of God's love in the Father, Son, and Holy Spirit.

> Let the same mind be in you
> that was in Christ Jesus,
> who, though he was in the form of God,
> did not regard equality with God
> as something to be exploited,
> but emptied himself,
> taking the form of a slave,
> being born in human likeness.
> And being found in human form,
> he humbled himself
> and became obedient to the point of death—
> even death on a cross.
>
> Therefore God also highly exalted him
> and gave him the name
> that is above every name,
> so that at the name of Jesus
> every knee should bend,
> in heaven and on earth and under the earth,
> and every tongue should confess
> that Jesus Christ is Lord,
> to the glory of God the Father.

Therefore, my beloved, just as you have always obeyed me, not only in my presence, but much more now in my absence, work out your own salvation with fear and trembling; for it is God who is at work in you, enabling you both to will and to work for his good pleasure.

Philippians 2:5-12

Gift of Clean Air

"The best things in life are free" goes the song. Air, oxygen, common wind, or whatever we name it is a gift supporting us in life as air-breathing earth creatures. Like the water and the sun we build a reverence for this special gift of God.

> Wild air, world-mothering air,
> Nestling me everywhere,
> That each eyelash or hair
> Girdles; goes home betwixt
> The fleeciest, frailest-flixed
> Snowflake; that's fairly mixed
> With riddles, and is rife
> In every least thing's life;
> This needful, never spent,
> And nursing element;
> My more than meat and drink,
> My meal at every wink;
> This air, which, by life's law,
> My lung must draw and draw
> Now but to breathe its praise. . . .

Gerard Manley Hopkins
Earth Prayers

PRAYER TWO

Thanks

As mysterious as it is, our belief of three persons in One God remains a basic element in our creed. Gratitude to God is always a thanksgiving prayer to the three persons of God: Father, Son, and Holy Spirit. This following community prayer of thanks artfully speaks for all Christians.

> For the bread that we have eaten
> For the wine that we have tasted
> For the life that you have given:
> Father, Son and Holy Spirit,
> We will praise you.
>
> For the life of Christ within us
> Turning all our fears to freedom
> Helping us to live for others:
> Father, Son and Holy Spirit,
> We will praise you.
>
> For the strength of Christ to lead us
> In our living and our dying,
> In the end with all your people
> Father, Son and Holy Spirit,
> We will praise you.

The Oxford Book of Prayers

A Buddhist Litany for Peace

Thich Nhat Hanh composed a prayer for peace that touches our souls whether our roots are warmly nestled in the East or West. This prayer serves as a beginning also for a longer meditation we may wish to exercise.

As we are together praying for Peace, let us be truly with each other.

Silence

Let us pay attention to our breathing.

Silence

Let us be relaxed in our bodies and our minds.

Silence

Let us be at peace with our bodies and our minds.

Silence

Let us return to ourselves and become wholly ourselves. Let us maintain a half-smile on our faces.

Silence

Let us be aware of the source of being common to us all and to all living things.

Silence

Evoking the presence of the Great Compassion, let us fill our hearts with our own compassion— towards ourselves and towards all living beings.

Silence

Let us pray that all living beings realize that they are all brothers and sisters, all nourished from the same source of life.

PRAYER THREE

Silence

Let us pray that we ourselves cease to be the cause of suffering to each other.

Silence

Let us plead with ourselves to live in a way which will not deprive other living beings of air, water, food, shelter, or the chance to live.

Silence

With humility, with awareness of the existence of life, and of the sufferings that are going on around us, let us pray for the establishment of peace in our hearts and on earth.

Amen.

The Venerable Thich Nhat Hanh in 1976

Drifting

Once, a very long time ago I was out on a large lake, in a fog, tired, alone, weather-pushed, and motorless. I was drifting and could not correct my plight. Suddenly I realized that all I was doing was lamenting and feeling sorry for myself. Struck with this feeling, I resonate with the words of Robert Byrne:

"The purpose of life is a life of purpose."

Ah . . . . drifter no longer!

Our Sacred Land

Spiritually we are all Jews receiving the promise of God to enter a land and a new life. This will be a land "flowing with milk and honey." The land itself symbolizes God's gifts—hidden and apparent.

The land ties us to all of nature as the gifts of God unfold daily in marvelous yet quite natural ways. We read in Deuteronomy:

> **For the LORD your God**
> **is bringing you**
> **into a good land,**
> **a land**
> **of flowing streams,**
> **with springs and underground waters**
> **welling up in valleys and hills,**
> **a land of wheat and barley,**
> **of vines and fig trees and pomegranates,**
> **a land of olive trees and honey,**
> **a land where you may eat bread without**
> **scarcity,**
> **where you will lack nothing,**
> **a land whose stones are iron**
> **and from whose hills you may mine copper.**
> **You shall eat your fill**
> **and bless the LORD your God**
> **for the good land**
> **he has given you.**

Deuteronomy 8:7-10

7. March Prayers

Lent and Lapsed Time
Rigors before the Resurrection

Kindness

Theodore Isaac Rubin remarked: "Kindness is more important than wisdom, and the recognition of this is the beginning of wisdom." Yet, there are some of us too busy with our developing projects and ascending careers to look to the work of kindness and the world of love. We see so often the world only as an opportunity for mastering all of the forces for growth other than those forces growing out of our deepest selves. Chardin said: "Some day, after we have mastered the winds, the waves, the tides and gravity we shall harness the energies of love. Then, for the second time in the history of the world, the human race will have discovered fire."

Random Acts of Kindness

PRAYER TWO

Nature

Longfellow provides soft transcendent glimpses of our natural process of living. As if by divine direction at each significant milestone along this path of life nature announces, ever so gently, our current position. In this process nature takes away our playthings in life, one by one, until nothing distracts us from our true purpose for moving along this path.

> As a fond mother, when the day is o'er,
>   Leads by the hand her little child to bed,
>   Half willing, half reluctant to be led,
>   And leave his broken playthings on the floor,
> Still gazing at them through the open door,
>   Nor wholly reassured and comforted
>   By promises of others in their stead,
>   Which, though more splendid, may not please
>   him more;
> So Nature deals with us, and takes away
>   Our playthings one by one, and by the hand
>   Leads us to rest so gently, that we go
> Scarce knowing if we wish to go or stay,
>   Being too full of sleep to understand
>   How far the unknown transcends what we
>   know.

Henry Wadsworth Longfellow (1807–1882)

Forgiveness

Connected with the funeral liturgy is the remarkable Psalm 130, called "From the Depths." The psalmist's prayer for God's forgiveness is readily understood as available to the faith-filled Jew. Repeating this psalm once again, we have yet one more opportunity to reflect on the role of forgiveness in God's life but also in the believer's life as he or she is expected to forgive others to certify the faith rooted in our forgiving God.

Out of the depths I cry to you, O LORD,
    Lord, hear my voice!
Let your ears be attentive
    to the voice of my supplications!

If you, O LORD, should mark iniquities,
    Lord, who could stand?
But there is forgiveness with you,
    so that you may be revered.

I wait for the LORD, my soul waits,
    and in his word I hope;
my soul waits for the Lord
    more than those who watch for the morning,
    more than those who watch for the morning.

O Israel, hope in the LORD!
    For with the LORD there is steadfast love,
    and with him is great power to redeem.
It is he who will redeem Israel
    from all its iniquities.

Psalm 130

Last Judgment

So much of what we do in this world is unimportant, yet in God's eyes some of what we do is significantly important. Always we are faced with the day-to-day actions we choose to perform for one or another reason. In Matthew's Gospel we read about those acts of a believer that truly matter in the eyes of God.

"When the Son of Man comes in his glory, and all the angels with him, then he will sit on the throne of his glory. All the nations will be gathered before him, and he will separate people one from another as a shepherd separates the sheep from the goats, and he will put the sheep at his right hand and the goats at the left. Then the king will say to those at his right hand, 'Come, you that are blessed by my Father, inherit the kingdom prepared for you from the foundation of the world; for I was hungry and you gave me food, I was thirsty and you gave me something to drink, I was a stranger and you welcomed me, I was naked and you gave me clothing, I was sick and you took care of me, I was in prison and you visited me.' Then the righteous will answer him, 'Lord, when was it that we saw you hungry and gave you food, or thirsty and gave you something to drink? And when was it that we saw you a stranger and welcomed you, or naked and gave you clothing? And when was it that we saw you sick or in prison and visited you?' And the king will answer them, 'Truly I tell you, just as you did it to one of the least of these who are members of my family, you did it to me.' Then he will say to those at his left hand, 'You that are accursed, depart from me into the eternal fire prepared for the devil and his angels; for I was hungry and you gave me no food, I was thirsty and you gave me nothing to drink, I was a stranger and you did not welcome me, naked and you did not give me clothing, sick and in prison and you did not visit me.' Then they will also answer, 'Lord, when was it that we saw you hungry or thirsty or a stranger or naked or sick or in prison, and did not take care of you?' Then he will answer them, 'Truly I tell you, just as you did not do it to one of the least of these, you did not do it to me.' And these will go away to eternal punishment, but the righteous into eternal life."

Matthew 25:31-46

Salvation

One operative word in religion is faith. We believe in someone whom we call God. We believe in God as the chief force in our lives. This belief leads to many other ideas such as patience, perseverance, and hope. These ideas lead further to the connection between God as parent, mother or father, and Christ as human-divine communicator between God and us. Paul unites these ideas in the following passage:

> **Therefore, since we are justified by faith, we have peace with God through our Lord Jesus Christ, through whom we have obtained access to this grace in which we stand; and we boast in our hope of sharing in the glory of God. And not only that, but we also boast in our sufferings, knowing that suffering produces endurance, and endurance produces character, and character produces hope, and hope does not disappoint us, because God's love has been poured into our hearts through the Holy Spirit that has been given to us.**
>
> **For while we were still weak, at the right time Christ died for the ungodly. Indeed, rarely will anyone die for a righteous person—though perhaps for a good person someone might actually dare to die. But God proves his love for us in that while we still were sinners Christ died for us.**
>
> *Romans 5:1-8*

Afterlife

Walt Whitman embraces a simple but awesome view of life after death. He calls us to reflect in our inevitable journey to that mysterious new position after life on earth as we now experience life.

> **What do you think has become of the young and**
>   **old men?**
> **And what do you think has become of the women**
>   **and children?**
>
> **They are alive and well somewhere,**
> **The smallest sprout shows there is really no death,**
> **And if ever there was it led forward life, and does**
>   **not wait at the end to arrest it,**
> **And ceas'd the moment life appear'd.**
>
> **All goes onward and outward, nothing collapses,**
> **And to die is different from what anyone supposed,**
>   **and luckier.**

From "Song of Myself"
Walt Whitman (1819–1892)

Inner Peace

Paul, the apostle, alerts us to the connection between inner peace and a sensitivity to those who are poor. At first glance, the two ideas appear to lack connection. But as we think about it further, the majority of the people on this planet are poor. To dismiss or disregard this majority would take us out of the mainstream of life. For Paul, peace must be found in the center of the mainstream, not on the fringes. We must be where all types of people live and work to note whether or not we practice charity to our neighbors.

Bless those who persecute you: bless and do not curse them. Rejoice with those who rejoice, weep with those who weep. Live in harmony with one another; do not be haughty, but associate with the lowly; do not claim to be wiser than you are. Do not repay anyone evil for evil, but take thought for what is noble in the sight of all. If it is possible, so far as it depends on you, live peaceably with all.

Romans 12:14-17

Suffering

To suffer at all in physical or natural terms is avoided by every normal human being. But, given the human condition, we all experience suffering in the course of a lifetime. Religion places the challenge to find meaning in suffering and grief. Paul urges us to look to God's will to explain our grieving.

> **For godly grief produces a repentance that leads to salvation and brings no regret, but worldly grief produces death.**
>
> *2 Corinthians 7:10*

Love as Followers of Christ

So much of life is mere talk, or as they say in politics, rhetoric. The Gospel of John alerts us to be "doers" of faith not mere talkers.

We know love by this, that he laid down his life for us—and we ought to lay down our lives for one another. How does God's love abide in anyone who has the world's goods and sees a brother or sister in need and yet refuses to help?

Little children, let us love, not in word or speech, but in truth and action.

1 John 3:16-18

Pass the Torch

Robert Bellah in *Habits of the Heart* reminds us that today, unfortunately, we have moved from community awareness to individual awareness. We are told, taught, and cajoled to value self above community. Well, we need to move beyond the classic argument of what is more important—the life of the community or the life of the individual. For now, we will pray over the quote of George Bernard Shaw.

> **"I am of the opinion that my life belongs to the community, and as long as I live, it is my privilege to do for it whatever I can. I want to be thoroughly used up when I die, for the harder I work, the more I live. Life is no "brief candle" to me. It is a sort of splendid torch which I have got hold of for a moment, and I want to make it burn as brightly as possible before handing it on to future generations."**

George Bernard Shaw

Another way of looking at this is shown to us by Herman Melville:

> **"We cannot live only for ourselves. A thousand fibers connect us with our fellow men; and among those fibers, as sympathetic threads, our actions run as causes, and they come back to us as effects."**

Herman Melville

God's Love and Mercy

Michael Fishbane says that biblical texts are selected again and again by us to draw out new understanding for our evolving life. As such, these texts are "rescued responses to the initiating presence and mystery of God in the course of human life."

One typical example of God inviting us through the repetitive prayer of the psalmist is Psalm 136. The Psalm is used in the time of sickness or distress, when God's work in our lives is not too clear.

O give thanks to the Lord, for he is good,
for his steadfast love endures forever.
O give thanks to the God of gods,
for his steadfast love endures forever.
O give thanks to the Lord of lords,
for his steadfast love endures forever;

who alone does great wonders,
for his steadfast love endures forever;
who by understanding made the heavens,
for his steadfast love endures forever;
who spread out the earth on the waters,
for his steadfast love endures forever;
who made the great lights,
for his steadfast love endures forever;
the sun to rule over the day,
for his steadfast love endures forever;
the moon and stars to rule over the night,
for his steadfast love endures forever;

who struck Egypt through their firstborn,
for his steadfast love endures forever;

and brought Israel out from among them,
    for his steadfast love endures forever;
with a strong hand and an outstretched arm,
    for his steadfast love endures forever;
who divided the Red Sea in two,
    for his steadfast love endures forever;
and made Israel pass through the midst of it,
    for his steadfast love endures forever;
but overthrew Pharaoh and his army in the Red Sea,
    for his steadfast love endures forever;
who led his people through the wilderness,
    for his steadfast love endures forever;
who struck down great kings,
    for his steadfast love endures forever;
and killed famous kings,
    for his steadfast love endures forever;
Sihon, king of the Amorites,
    for his steadfast love endures forever;
and Og, king of Bashan,
    for his steadfast love endures forever;
and gave their land as a heritage,
    for his steadfast love endures forever;
a heritage to his servant Israel,
    for his steadfast love endures forever;

It is he who remembered us in our low estate,
    for his steadfast love endures forever;
and rescued us from our foes,
    for his steadfast love endures forever;
who gives food to all flesh,
    for his steadfast love endures forever;

O give thanks to the God of heaven,
    for his steadfast love endures forever.

Psalm 136

Count Down

When we are sixteen, the world is called future. Everything is before us—adventure, career, marriage, family, success, etc. But, . . . who knows? So we hear Marcus Aurelius urge us:

"Do every act of your life as if it were your last."

Death as a Loss

W. H. Auden speaks for us when he tells of suffering the loss of a dear friend. Here Auden gives us a prayer that we can carry to the throne of God and ask for an understanding of the meaning of Good Friday.

But in the importance and noise of tomorrow
When the brokers are roaring like beasts on the
   floor of the Bourse,
And the poor have the sufferings to which they are
   fairly accustomed,
And each in the cell of himself is almost convinced
   of his freedom;
A few thousand will think of this day
As one thinks of a day when one did something
   slightly unusual.

O all the instruments agree
The day of his death was a dark cold day.

From "In Memory of W. B. Yeats"
W. H. Auden (1907–)

Prayer for Conservation

Care among human beings is a mutual enterprise. We help others so that we may hope that they in turn will help us when we are in need. This principle is true also in our relation to the earth as linked to a life of reciprocal esteem.

Great Spirit,
give us hearts to understand,
never to take
from creation's beauty more than we give,
never to destroy wantonly for the furtherance of
greed;
never to deny to give our hands for the building of
earth's beauty;
never to take from her what we cannot use.
Give us hearts to understand that to destroy earth's
music is to create confusion;
that to wreck her appearance is to blind us to
beauty;
that to callously pollute her fragrance is to make a
house of stench;
that as we care for her she will care for us. Amen.

U.N. Environmental Sabbath Program
Earth Prayers

Suffering and Joy

"It is possible to decrease the suffering in the world by adding to the joy. It is possible to add to the light rather than trying to destroy the darkness. Once you begin to acknowledge random acts of kindness—both the ones you have received and the ones you have given—you can no longer believe that what you do does not matter."

The above quote from *Random Acts of Kindness* brings the word "random" into a new light. We ask ourselves the question: "Are we trained to think only of deficits, notice only people's faults, reflect only on human suffering?"

The Gospels and people who have lived the Gospels such as Maya Angelou, Mother Teresa, and Pope John XXIII tell us we can and do make a difference. WE CAN DO!

Goodness of God

SOMETIMES it is difficult to recognize the goodness of God in the face of overwhelming human suffering.

This understanding is expressed in the beautiful but simple prayer of a Breton fisherman who said:

> **DEAR GOD: be good to me:**
> **The sea is so wide,**
> **And my boat is so small.**
>
> **Amen.**

Love—Compassion—Forgiveness

Tied to love is the virtue of forgiveness. Paul sees God's love for us as a basic motive for developing compassion and patience as we daily interact with our fellow human beings.

As God's chosen ones holy and beloved, clothe yourselves with compassion, kindness, humility, meekness, and patience. Bear with one another and, if anyone has a complaint against another, forgive each other; just as the Lord has forgiven you, so you also must forgive. Above all, clothe yourselves with love, which binds everything together in perfect harmony. And let the peace of Christ rule in your hearts, to which indeed you were called in the one body.

Colossians 3:12-15

Spirit of God

The Spirit of God in the trinitarian sense is the Holy Spirit. This word spirit means breath, and wind, and air, and mystical force that gives life and sustenance to all it touches. Strangely enough the Southern Bushmen called on that spirit to serve as the power closing the book of our lives by taking away our footprints in the desert of life. This prayer stands in stark contrast to the mind of those who feel they must leave their mark on this earth before they leave it.

The day we die
the wind comes down
to take away
our footprints.

The wind makes dust
to cover up
the marks we left
while walking.

For otherwise
the thing would seem
as if we were
still living.

Therefore the wind
is he who comes
to blow away
our footprints.

Southern Bushmen
Earth Prayers

God's Grandeur

When we wear shoes we do not feel the various seams and pockets of the ground. We do not feel the difference when we move from dirt to asphalt to cement as we walk ever onward towards our goals. Yet in many places in the United States kids still run barefoot during the summer and sensitize their feet to the pebbles and clay and grass and cement that meets them as they move through their vacation days.

Gerard Manley Hopkins sees God's grandeur in this pedestrian experience.

> **The world is charged with the grandeur of God.**
> **It will flame out, like shining from shook foil;**
> **It gathers to a greatness, like the ooze of oil**
> **Crushed. Why do men then now not reck his rod?**
> **Generation have trod, have trod, have trod;**
> **And all is seared with trade; bleared, smeared with toil;**
> **And wears man's smudge and shares man's smell: the soil**
> **Is bare now, nor can foot feel, being shod.**
> **And for all this, nature is never spent;**
> **There lives the dearest freshness deep down things;**
> **And though the last lights off the black West went**
> **Oh, morning, at the brown brink eastward, springs—**
> **Because the Holy Ghost over the bent**
> **World broods with warm breast and with ah! bright wings.**

Gerard Manley Hopkins (1844–1889)

The Medal

Raising children might just be the greatest challenge to any adult. Each parent or guardian tries to draw a child to truth in direct and pleasant ways without distressing detours based on fear. Anthony de Mello tells the following story:

Man finds himself alone and lost in this vast universe. And he is full of fears.

Good religion makes him fearless. Bad religion increases his fears.

A mother could not get her little son to come home from his games before dusk. So she frightened him: she told him that the path leading to their house was haunted by ghosts who came out as soon as the sun went down. She had no more trouble making him come home in time each evening.

But when the boy grew up he was so afraid of the dark and of ghosts that he refused to get out of the house at night. So she gave him a medal to wear and convinced him that as long as he wore his medal the ghosts would have no power to harm him.

So now he ventures forth into the dark clutching his medal.

Bad religion strengthens his faith in the medal. Good religion gets him to see that there are no ghosts.

The Song of the Bird

8. April Prayers

*Cool to Warmer
Mixed Sun and Showers
Celebration and Joy*

Day-by-Day, *Anima Christi:*

We will consider a double-prayer today. The first comes from the musical *Godspell* and it is entitled "Day-by-Day." The second prayer is the *Anima Christi,* used as a prayer after the reception of Holy Communion. Each prayer complements the other as suited to the beginning of each day.

> Lord,
> "May I know you more clearly,
> Love you more dearly,
> And follow you more nearly,
> Day by day."

> Soul of Christ, sanctify me.
> Body of Christ, save me.
> Blood of Christ, inebriate me.
> Water from the side of Christ, wash me.
> Passion of Christ, strengthen me.
> O Good Jesus, hear me.
> Within thy wounds hide me.
> Permit me not to be separated from thee.
> From the wicked foe defend me.
> At the hour of death call me
> and bid me come to thee,
> that with all the saints I may praise thee
> forever and ever.

> Amen.

Order and Chaos in this World

Sometimes it is important that we know where the "boss" is. She can be moving around the plant, or she might be sitting in her office, but when we ask "is everything running properly," we are consoled to hear that the "boss is in her office and able to be reached by her secretary." On a cosmic level (comparing plant with planet), we ask similar questions: "Who is in charge? Is everything okay?"

Robert Browning consoles us in this brief passage from "Pippa Passes":

> **The year's at the spring**
> **And day's at the morn;**
> **Morning's at seven;**
> **The hill-side's dew-pearled;**
> **The lark's on the wing;**
> **The snail's on the thorn;**
> **God's in his heaven—**
> **All's right with the world!**

Robert Browning (1812–1889)

You Are a Marvel

Beyond dictionary definitions we slowly learn what human persons are and, consequently, who we are. The process of learning is a gift. The following passage offers a reflective boost to our learning process.

Each second we live is a new and unique moment of the universe, a moment that will never be again . . . And what do we teach our children? We teach them that two and two make four, and that Paris is the capital of France.

When will we also teach them what they are?

We should say to each of them: Do you know what you are? You are a marvel. You are unique. In all the years that have passed, there has never been another child like you. Your legs, your arms, your clever fingers, the way you move.

You may become a Shakespeare, a Michelangelo, a Beethoven. You have the capacity for anything. Yes, you are a marvel. And when you grow up, can you then harm another who is, like you, a marvel?

You must work—we all must work—to make the world worthy of its children.

Pablo Casals
from Chicken Soup for the Soul

I AM

Helen Mallicoat suggests the following prayer for those of us who find difficulty living in the present time:

I was regretting the past and fearing the future. Suddenly my Lord was speaking:

"My name is I AM." He passed. I waited. He continued. "When you live in the past, with its mistakes and regrets, it is hard. I am not there. My name is not I WAS. When you live in the future, with its problems and fears, it is hard. I am not there. My name is not I WILL BE. When you live in this moment, it is not hard. I am here. My name is I AM."

Helen Mallicoat

Mystery of God and Life

Everyone would be pleased to know who God is. This enduring and, at times, overwhelming mystery of God stalks us at every turn in our life's journey. Hence, Tennyson remarks about a very limited and fragile understanding of God through nature that intrigues us. His sensitivity becomes for us a prayer.

> **Flower in the crannied wall,**
> **I pluck you out of the crannies,**
> **I hold you here, root and all, in my hand,**
> **Little flower—but if I could understand**
> **What you are, root and all, and all in all,**
> **I should know what God and man is.**

> *"Flower in the Crannied Wall"*
> *Alfred Tennyson (1809–1892)*

Worry

Psychologists remind us that worry never assists us as we face life's problems. We have at times a need for concern about human obligations and how to fulfill them, but worry and concern are as different as pneumonia and a slight cold.

In the Sermon on the Mount, Matthew highlights the limits of worry in our spiritual life.

> "Therefore I tell you, do not worry about your life, what you will eat or what you will drink, or about your body, what you will wear. Is not life more than food, and the body more than clothing? Look at the birds of the air; they neither sow nor reap nor gather into barns, and yet your heavenly Father feeds them. Are you not of more value than they? And can any of you by worrying add a single hour to your span of life? And why do you worry about clothing? Consider the lilies of the field, how they grow; they neither toil nor spin, yet I tell you, even Solomon in all his glory was not clothed like one of these. But if God so clothes the grass of the field, which is alive today and tomorrow is thrown into the oven, will he not much more clothe you—you of little faith? Therefore do not worry, saying, 'What will we eat?' or 'What will we drink?' or 'What will we wear?' For it is the Gentiles who strive for all these things; and indeed your heavenly Father knows that you need all these things. But strive first for the kingdom of God and his righteousness, and all these things will be given to you as well.

"So do not worry about tomorrow, for tomorrow will bring worries of its own. Today's trouble is enough for today."

Matthew 6:25-34

Institution of the Eucharist

The clearest description of what Jesus said at the Last Supper when he instituted the Eucharist is found in Paul's First Letter to the Corinthians.

> **For I received from the Lord what I also handed on to you, that the Lord Jesus on the night when he was betrayed took a loaf of bread, and when he had given thanks, he broke it and said, "This is my body that is for you. Do this in remembrance of me." In the same way he took the cup also, after supper, saying, "This cup is the new covenant in my blood. Do this, as often as you drink it, in remembrance of me." For as often as you eat this bread and drink the cup, you proclaim the Lord's death until he comes.**
>
> *1 Corinthians 11:23-26*

Happiness

"The only ones among you who will be really happy are those who have sought and found a way to serve."

Albert Schweitzer

Somehow service flows from a love that is developed over the years. St. Augustine says:

What does love look like?
It has feet to go to the poor and needy.
It has eyes to see misery and want.
It has ears to hear the sighs and sorrows of others.

Vision 2000

Truth

The mottos on the coats of arms of many educational institutions tell of the constant academic search for truth. How often you and I fail to seek out the truth that is in ourselves—our hearts, our personalities. John's Gospel records optimistically:

"You will know the truth and the truth will make you free."

John 8:32

William Shakespeare many centuries later adds:

"This above all
to thine own self be true
And it must follow,
As the night the day
Thou canst not then be false to any man."

Hamlet (Act 1, Scene 3)

Gentleness

Ralph Waldo Emerson said: "What you are speaks so loudly, I can't hear what you are saying." Jesus taught not only by words but especially by his actions. When we seek advice or consolation from Jesus, we can go to the Scriptures, especially to the following passage:

> **"Come to me, all you that are weary and are carrying heavy burdens, and I will give you rest. Take my yoke upon you, and learn from me; for I am gentle and humble in heart, and you will find rest for your souls."**

> *Matthew 11:28, 29*

The Lord's Prayer

When Hollywood discovered that it could use slow-motion in films to heighten dramatic effect, a whole new way of directing films evolved.

When you and I pray, often we realize we must first slow down to open our hearts to the effects God wishes to produce. For a change of pace let us recite together the Our Father, but let us say it ever so slowly, pausing slightly after each phrase. Allow me to lead this prayer and set the pace. Please chime in.

> **Our Father, who art in heaven,**
> **hallowed be thy name;**
> **Thy kingdom come;**
> **Thy will be done on earth as it is in heaven.**
> **Give us this day our daily bread;**
> **and forgive us our trespasses**
> **as we forgive those who trespass against us;**
> **and lead us not into temptation,**
> **but deliver us from evil.**
> **For the kingdom, the power and the glory are**
>   **yours,**
> **now and forever. Amen.**

Humility

My old philosophy professor once said that teachers should be humble because in reality it only takes one phone call to replace a teacher. He added gently: "But it takes two phone calls to replace a philosophy professor." An anonymous poem reads:

> **When you're feeling so important,**
> **And your ego is in bloom,**
> **When you simply take for granted**
> **You're the wisest in the room,**
> **When you feel your very absence**
> **Would leave a great big hole,**
> **Just follow these instructions.**
> **They will humble any soul.**
> **Take a bucket filled with water**
> **Put your hand in to the wrist,**
> **Pull it out, the hole remaining**
> **Is how much you will be missed. . . .**

Vision 2000

Perfection—Faith in Christ

We pray to be perfect in God's eyes. Moreover, we pray that we recognize that perfection does not come merely by following laws and rules. Our perfection comes from our faith in God. Paul reviews these ideas in his Letter to the Philippians.

> Yet whatever gains I had, these I have come to regard as loss because of Christ. More than that, I regard everything as loss because of the surpassing value of knowing Christ Jesus as my Lord. For his sake I have suffered the loss of all things, and I regard them as rubbish, in order that I may gain Christ and be found in him, not having a righteousness of my own that comes from the law, but one that comes through faith in Christ, the righteousness from God based on faith.
>
> *Philippians 3:7-9*

Revelation of God

Mark Link tells the following story:

> A "puzzle page" in the newspaper showed a drawing of an outdoor scene. Beneath it was this question: "Can you find the girl in the drawing?" A close examination of the drawing showed the girl's eyes and eyebrows concealed in a tree branch. Another branch hid her mouth and nose. A cloud revealed her flowing hair. After you discovered the girl, that drawing was never the same again.
>
> Vision 2000

It is like that with God. God is always there in our lives waiting to be found. Once we find him, our picture of the world will never be the same again.

PRAYER FIVE

An Indian Prayer

The North American native possessed a deep spirituality much to the surprise of the exploitative immigrants from Europe. Somehow, even in the acceptance of Christianity, a deep spirituality tied to the pre-Christian ancestors remains.

O Great Spirit,
Whose voice I hear in the winds,
And whose breath gives life to all the world,
hear me! I am small and weak, I need your
strength and wisdom.

Let Me Walk in Beauty, and make my eyes
ever behold the red and purple sunset.

Make My Hands respect the things you have
made and my ears sharp to hear your voice.

Make Me Wise so that I may understand the
things you have taught my people.

Let Me Learn the lessons you have hidden
in every leaf and rock.

I Seek Strength, not to be greater than my
brother, but to fight my greatest enemy—myself.

Make Me Always Ready to come to you with
clean hands and straight eyes.

So When Life Fades, as the fading sunset,
my spirit may come to you without shame.

If I Had My Life Over

For so many of us life is filled with regrets, and mental 20/20 hindsight. Thinking positively contributes to our present well-being, but admittedly, it is quite difficult! Nadine Stair lends a helping hand by her words:

I'd dare to make more mistakes next time. I'd relax, I would limber up. I would be sillier than I have been this trip. I would take fewer things seriously. I would take more chances. I would climb more mountains and swim more rivers. I would eat more ice cream and less beans. I would perhaps have more actual troubles, but I'd have fewer imaginary ones.

You see, I'm one of those people who live sensibly and sanely hour after hour, day after day. Oh, I've had my moments, and if I had it to do over again, I'd have more of them. In fact, I'd try to have nothing else. Just moments, one after another, instead of living so many years ahead of each day. I've been one of those persons who never goes anywhere without a thermometer, a hot water bottle, a raincoat and a parachute. If I had to do it again, I would travel lighter than I have.

If I had my life to live over, I would start barefoot earlier in the spring and stay that way later in the fall. I would go to more dances. I would ride more merry-go-rounds. I would pick more daisies.

Prayer

St. Benedict used a famous maxim as a central support to the entire Benedictine life. He said "pray and work" *(ora et labora)*. Strangely enough the simple coordinating conjunction is pivotal to this statement. *And* is used to show an equal balance between what went before and what follows. Prayer alone or work alone is insufficient. St. Ignatius said it another way:

Work as though all depends on you.
Pray as though all depends on God.

Eucharist

The word "Eucharist" means "thank you." Part of the mystery of this sacrament is brought home by the actual experience of the liturgy. On those quiet Sunday mornings we Christians gather together to pray over the meaning of the gift of Christ among us.

> **We asked Jesus for a grain of sand,**
> **he gave us a beach.**
> **We asked him for a drop of water,**
> **he gave us an ocean.**
> **We asked him for his love,**
> **he gave us his body and blood.**

Mark Link
Vision 2000

Songs of Praise

Sometimes it is beneficial to pray aloud as a community. The ancient prayers of the Jews as well as later Christians allowed for this antiphonal praying. Let us examine a psalm for our prayer today.

Praise the LORD!
Praise God in his sanctuary;
 praise him in his mighty firmament!
Praise him for his mighty deeds;
 praise him according to his surpassing greatness!

Praise him with trumpet sound;
 praise him with lute and harp!
Praise him with tambourine and dance;
 praise him with strings and pipe!
Praise him with clanging cymbals;
 praise him with loud clashing cymbals!
Let everything that breathes praise the LORD!
Praise the LORD!

Psalm 150

To Know Christ

So much of religious education for a Christian is geared to learning about Jesus Christ. But many of us admit we do not have the skills to really know Christ. Anthony de Mello expands on this idea.

A dialogue between a recent convert to Christ and an unbelieving friend:

"So you have been converted to Christ?"
"Yes"
"Then you must know a great deal about him. Tell me: what country was he born in?"
"I don't know."
"What was his age when he died?"
"I don't know."
"How many sermons did he preach?"
"I don't know."
"You certainly know very little for a man who claims to be converted to Christ!"
"You are right. I am ashamed of how little I know about him. But this much I do know: three years ago I was a drunkard. I was in debt. My family was falling to pieces. My wife and children would dread my return home each evening. But now I have given up drink; we are out of debt; ours is now a happy home; my children eagerly wait for my return home each evening. All this Christ has done for me. This much I know of Christ!"

To *really* know. That is, to be transformed by what one knows.

The Song of the Bird

9. May Prayers

*Warm Wind of the Spirit and Ready
Resolve of the Students to Seek a
Successful Year's Conclusion*

The Holy Spirit

The liturgy of Pentecost reminds us that the Spirit is in charge of our lives and the lives of the entire world community. Fortunately, we have the following prayer taken from the Pentecost liturgy to serve as a solid reminder of the work of the Spirit.

> Come, thou Holy Spirit, come! And from thy
>   celestial home
>   Shed a ray of light divine!
> Come, thou Father of the poor! Come, thou source
>   of all our store!
>   Come, within our bosoms shine!
> Thou, of comforters the best; Thou the soul's most
>   welcome guest;
>   Sweet refreshments here below;
> In our labor, rest most sweet; grateful coolness in
>   the heat;
>   Solace in the midst of woe.
> O most blessed light divine, Shine within these
>   hearts of thine,
>   And our inmost being fill!
> Where thou art not, we have naught, Nothing good
>   in deed or thought,
>   Nothing free from taint of ill.
> Heal our wounds, our strength renew; On our
>   dryness pour thy dew;
>   Wash the stains of guilt away:
> Bend the stubborn heart and will; Melt the frozen,
>   warm the chill;
>   Guide the steps that go astray.
> On the faithful, who adore And confess thee,
>   evermore

In the sevenfold gift descend;
Give them virtue's sure reward; Give them thy sal-
vation, Lord;
Give them joys that never end. Amen. Alleluia.

Oxford Book of Prayers

To Be a Part of Life

Our identity is tied to our surroundings. As North Americans we display certain attitudes and inclinations. We take our past forward and we are what we experience. Never can we deny our own personal history and the atmosphere that has contributed to that history.

Tennyson says:

> I am a part of all that I have met;
> Yet all experience is an arch wherethrough
> Gleams that untraveled world, whose margin fades
> Forever and forever when I move.
> How dull it is to pause, to make an end,
> to rust unburnished, not to shine in use!

From "Ulysses"
Alfred Tennyson (1808–1892)

Searching for God

Anthony de Mello remarks how the most reputable theologian of Christian history changed his style after a distinct religious experience.

The story goes that Thomas Aquinas, one of the world's ablest theologians, suddenly stopped writing towards the end of his life. When his secretary complained that his work was unfinished, Thomas replied: "Brother Reginald, when I was celebrating the liturgy some months ago I experienced something of the Divine. That day I lost all appetite for writing. In fact, all I have ever written about God seems to me now to be like straw."

How could it be otherwise when the scholar becomes a mystic?

The Song of the Bird

The Ocean

In Washington we have the privilege of living next to the Pacific Ocean. By contrast to the plains and mountains, the ocean lies beyond most powers of human control. We do a lamentable job of polluting the ocean, but ultimately the ocean will outlive our species. Meanwhile, should the ocean take us, we lose the consolation of a traditional burial in the ground with family and friends standing around our grave mourning our sudden departure. George Gordon, Lord Byron, reveals his awesome awareness of this formidable power, the ocean.

> **Roll on, thou deep and dark blue Ocean—roll!**
> **Ten thousand fleets sweep over thee in vain;**
> **Man marks the earth with ruin; his control**
> **Stops with the shore; upon the watery plain**
> **The wrecks are all thy deed, nor doth remain**
> **A shadow of man's ravage, save his own,**
> **When for a moment, like a drop of rain,**
> **He sinks into thy depths with bubbling groan,**
> **Without a grave, unknelled, uncoffined and**
>   **unknown.**

George Gordon, Lord Byron (1788–1824)

God's Love

St. Augustine reminds us that God is closer and more intimate to us than we are to ourselves. The prophet Isaiah in chapter 43 reminds us of our place in God's love.

**Do not fear, for I have redeemed you;
 I have called you by name, you are mine . . .**

**You are precious in my sight,
 and honored, and I love you . . .**

Do not fear, for I am with you.

Isaiah 43:1, 4, 5

God Described as Father, Son, and Spirit—Helping Us

Much of what we are is hidden. For years it is hidden from ourselves. In time, we discover our hidden gifts, then it remains hidden only from others who fail to call upon us in a spirit of charity. Once the Spirit of God lives in us we are able to serve God effectively by reaching out to our neighbor. The Letter to the Ephesians gives us this trinitarian meditation.

For this reason I bow my knees before the Father, from whom every family in heaven and on earth takes its name. I pray that, according to the riches of his glory, he may grant that you may be strengthened in your inner being with power through his Spirit, and that Christ may dwell in your hearts through faith, as you are being rooted and grounded in love. I pray that you may have the power to comprehend, with all the saints, what is the breadth and length and height and depth, and to know the love of Christ that surpasses knowledge, so that you may be filled with all the fullness of God.

Ephesians 3:14-19

Change

Self-help books in our individualistic age urge us to be fulfilled, to seek to actualize our human potential, to be all we can. All of this self-centered growth implies change. The question is: "Is it a change for the better?" The direction of change and fulfillment Christ offered was slightly different. He said:

"Unless you change and become like children, you will never enter the kingdom of heaven."

Matthew 18:3

Call of Jeremiah as Elemental to All Vocations

Jeremiah reveals how God called him to prophecy and promised special protection during Jeremiah's service. This passage evokes reflection in each of us as we respond to God in our personal vocations to live out our lives.

Now the word of the LORD came to me saying,
"Before I formed you in the womb I knew you,
and before you were born I consecrated you;
I appointed you a prophet to the nations."
Then I said, "Ah, Lord God! Truly I do not know
how to speak, for I am only a boy." But the LORD
said to me,
"Do not say, 'I am only a boy';
for you shall go to all to whom I send you,
and you shall speak whatever I command you,
Do not be afraid of them,
for I am with you to deliver you,
says the LORD."

Jeremiah 1:4-8

Let the Day Come, Lord

Archbishop Oscar Romero wrote several prayers in the last two years of his life before being assassinated in El Salvador. One example is:

> **Come, Lord Jesus, come!**
>
> **Let the day come, Lord,**
> **when our misery**
> **will find your mercy.**
>
> **Let the day come, Lord**
> **when our poverty**
> **will find your riches.**
>
> **Let the day come, Lord**
> **when our path**
> **will find the way to your house.**
>
> **Let the day come, Lord**
> **when our tears**
> **will find your smile.**
>
> **Let the day come, Lord**
> **when our joy**
> **will find your heaven.**
>
> **Let the day come, Lord**
> **when your Church**
> **will find your Kingdom.**
>
> **May you be blest, Father,**
> **for that day**
> **when our eyes will find your face!**
> **Throughout all the time of our life**

you have not ceased to come before us
  in your Son Jesus Christ,
our Savior and our brother.

Love

The simple identity of God and love gives deeper understanding to both words although each remains mysterious in its transcendent power. The First Letter of John alerts us to the connection between God and love.

Beloved, let us love one another, because love is from God; everyone who loves is born of God and knows God. Whoever does not love does not know God, for God is love.

1 John 4:7-8

Variety of Gifts

Some of us get carried away with our own unique talents and gifts, until we realize that all of our talents or unique gifts come from God our creator. Paul says:

Now there are varieties of gifts, but the same Spirit; and there are varieties of services, but the same Lord; and there are varieties of activities, but it is the same God who activates all of them in everyone. To each is given the manifestation of the Spirit for the common good. To one is given through the Spirit the utterance of wisdom, and to another the utterance of knowledge according to the same Spirit, to another faith by the same Spirit, to another gifts of healing by the one Spirit, to another the working of miracles, to another prophecy, to another the discernment of spirits, to another various kinds of tongues, to another the interpretation of tongues. All these are activated by one and the same Spirit, who allots to each one individually just as the Spirit chooses.

1 Corinthians 12:4-11

Prayer for the Sick and Troubled

The traditional text cited for the development of the sacrament of the Anointing of the Sick is chapter 5 of the Letter of James. This passage connects faith with healing and allows for all sorts of results from God's grace, even the restraint of a physical cure in favor of a deeper spiritual awakening. Finally, the help one sinner gives to another is considered a means of receiving forgiveness for one's own sins.

Are there any among you suffering? They should pray. Are any cheerful? They should sing songs of praise. Are any among you sick? They should call for the elders of the church and have them pray over them, anointing them with oil in the name of the Lord. The prayer of faith will save the sick, and the Lord will raise them up; and anyone who has committed sins will be forgiven. Therefore confess your sins to one another, and pray for one another, so that you may be healed. The prayer of the righteous is powerful and effective. Elijah was a human being like us, and he prayed fervently that it might not rain, and for three years and six months it did not rain on the earth. Then he prayed again, and the heaven gave rain and the earth yielded its harvest.

My brothers and sisters, if anyone among you wanders from the truth and is brought back by another, you should know that whoever brings back a sinner from wandering will save the sinner's soul from death and will cover a multitude of sins.

James 5:13-20

Hope in Time of Sorrow

Every human being has dignity that speaks courageously at all times. We need not accomplish great things to show our dignity. Merely to be is to have dignity.

I am: yet what I am none cares or knows,
    My friends forsake me like a memory lost;
I am the self-consumer of my woes,
    They rise and vanish in oblivious host,
Like shades in love and death's oblivion lost;
And yet I am, and live with shadows lost.

Into the nothingness of scorn and noise,
    Into the living sea of waking dreams,
Where there is neither sense of life nor joys,
    But the vast shipwreck of my life's esteems;
And e'en the dearest—that I loved the best—
Are strange—nay, rather stranger than the rest.

I long for scenes where man has never trod;
    A place where woman never smiled or wept;
There to abide with my Creator, God,
    And sleep as I in childhood sweetly slept:
Untroubling and untroubled where I lie;
The grass below—above the vaulted sky.

"I Am"
Written in Northampton County Asylum
John Clare (1793–1864)

219

PRAYER FOUR

God in Nature

Wordsworth talks of taking time out to listen to nature as nature speaks of God. Here in the Northwest we often go out into the untraveled paths of our wonderful atmosphere simply to listen as God speaks to us.

Wordsworth says:

> For I have learned
> To look on Nature, not as in the hour
> Of thoughtless youth; but hearing oftentimes
> The still, sad music of humanity,
> Nor harsh nor grating, though of ample power
> To chasten and subdue. And I have felt
> A presence that disturbs me with the joy
> Of elevated thoughts; a sense sublime
> Of something far more deeply interfused,
> Whose dwelling is the light of setting suns,
> And the round ocean and the living air,
> And the blue sky, and in the mind of man;
> A motion and a spirit, that impels
> All thinking things, all objects of all thought,
> And rolls through all things.

William Wordsworth
"Lines, Composed a Few Miles
Above Tintern Abbey . . ." (1798)

Serenity

Reinhold Niebuhr stands as one of the most famous theologians of the twentieth century. His most famous prayer is a simple and ubiquitous statement that is rarely associated with his name.

"God, grant me the serenity to accept the things I cannot change, courage to change the things I can, and wisdom to know the difference."

Wrestle with God

As Christians and Jews we believe that we are children of Abraham, Isaac, and Jacob. We believe they are our ancestors who historically handed down to us our faith, God-given though it is. Strangely enough, Jacob's name was changed. God changed Jacob's name because one evening Jacob confronted God, talked and debated with Him, and eventually wrestled with God. For this reason God changed Jacob's name to ISRAEL which means, "One who wrestles with God." As we read the passage below recounting the story, we can reflect that as children of Jacob, we are Israelites; we have the right to wrestle, spiritually at least, with God. We always keep in mind that each encounter with God is prompted by love and devotion.

> The same night he got up and took his two wives, his two maids, and his eleven children, and crossed the ford of the Jabbok. He took them and sent them across the stream, and likewise everything that he had. Jacob was left alone; and a man wrestled with him until daybreak. When the man saw that he did not prevail against Jacob, he struck him on the hip socket; and Jacob's hip was put out of joint as he wrestled with him. Then he said, "Let me go, for the day is breaking." But Jacob said, "I will not let you go, unless you bless me." So he said to him, "What is your name?" And he said, "Jacob." Then the man said, "You shall no longer be called Jacob, but Israel, for you have striven with God and with humans, and have prevailed." Then Jacob asked him, "Please tell me your name." But he said, "Why is it that you ask my name?" And there he blessed him.

Genesis 32:22-29

Gaelic Blessing

In gift shops around the world we find this Irish blessing that speaks the heart of all nationalities.

> **May the road rise to meet you.**
> **May the wind be always at your back.**
> **May the sun shine warm upon your face.**
> **May the rains fall softly upon your fields**
> **until we meet again.**
> **May God hold you in the hollow of his hand.**

Old Gaelic blessing

Human Dignity

Two dangers as if in opposition to one another confront us as we consider the dignity of human life:

> **To make human life the center and goal of the universe (i.e. anthropocentrism), or, because of our late entrance into the universe, to give highest honor to the stars and galaxies in the universe because of their sheer resplendent vastness.**

Ian Barbour reminds us:

> **There are a hundred trillion synapses in a human brain; the number of possible ways of connecting them is greater than the number of atoms in the universe. A higher level of organization and a greater richness of experience occurs in a human beings than in a thousand lifeless galaxies.**

Lest we confuse this complexity with the goal of the universe, Barbour continues:

> **The chemical elements in your hand and in your brain were forged in the furnace of the stars. The cosmos is all of a piece. It is multileveled; each new higher level was built on lower levels from the past. Humanity is the most advanced form of life we know, but it is fully a part of a wider process in space and time.**

> *Religion in an Age of Science*

Water

Water, a gift, and duty, a human condition, mix in the reflective prayer of Thich Nhat Hanh.

Water flows from high in the mountains
    Water runs deep in the Earth
Miraculously, water comes to us,
    and sustains all life.

Water flows over these hands
May I use them skillfully
to preserve our precious planet.

Thich Nhat Hanh
Earth Prayers

Faith in the Eucharist

It is seemingly unreasonable to believe that eating a wafer of bread or drinking a sip of wine will bring everlasting life to a human person. Yet, once we are convinced Jesus is divine and will give us a share in his life through the eucharistic bread and wine we enter the realm of faith that connects our mind and heart with the direct revelation of the Son of God.

The tradition of John opens up the implications of this eucharistic faith.

> **"No one can come to me unless drawn by the Father who sent me; and I will raise that person up on the last day. It is written in the prophets, 'And they shall all be taught by God.' Everyone who has heard and learned from the Father comes to me. Not that anyone has seen the Father except the one who is from God; he has seen the Father. Very truly, I tell you, whoever believes has eternal life. I am the bread of life. Your ancestors ate the manna in the wilderness, and they died. This is the bread that comes down from heaven, so that one may eat of it and not die. I am the living bread that came down from heaven. Whoever eats of this bread will live forever; and the bread that I will give for the life of the world is my flesh."**

> *John 6:44-51*

Index

The subject references indicate the month with a (1st), (2nd), (3rd), or (4th) after the month to indicate the week.